MATH MANIA

DOVER PUBLICATIONS, INC.
MINEOLA, NEW YORK

education.com

Bibliographical Note

Math Mania, first published by Dover Publications, Inc., in 2015, contains pages from
the following online workbooks published by Education.com: *Master Multiplication, Fun
with Fractions, Learn Fractions and Decimals,* and *Operations Practice.*

International Standard Book Number
ISBN-13: 978-0-486-80271-8
ISBN-10: 0-486-80271-X

Manufactured in the United States by Courier Corporation
80271X01   2015
www.doverpublications.com

CONTENTS

Master Multiplication 1

Fun with Fractions 27

Learn Fractions and Decimals 51

Operations Practice 69

Answers 87

CONTENTS

Master Multiplication ....
Fun with Fractions 27
Learn Fractions and Decimals 51
Operations Practice 69
Answers 82

Master Multiplication

Addition Facts

Multiplication problems can also be expressed with addition. Write the addition facts that go with each multiplication sentence. The first one is done for you.

3 x 7 = _3 + 3 + 3 + 3 + 3 + 3 + 3_

5 x 4 = _____

6 x 2 = _____

10 x 5 = _____

7 x 7 = _____

9 x 4 = _____

Look at the pictures below.

Write the addition fact: _____

Write the multiplication sentence: _____

Making Multiplication Sentences

Look at each picture below. Write both the addition and multiplication facts that illustrate each picture. The first one is done for you.

2 + 2 + 2 _____

2 x 3 = 6 _____

_____

_____

_____

_____

_____

_____

_____

_____

Making Multiplication Sentences

Kick off! Time to take the field and score a touchdown for the home team. Solve the following multiplication problems and you'll be an All-Pro!

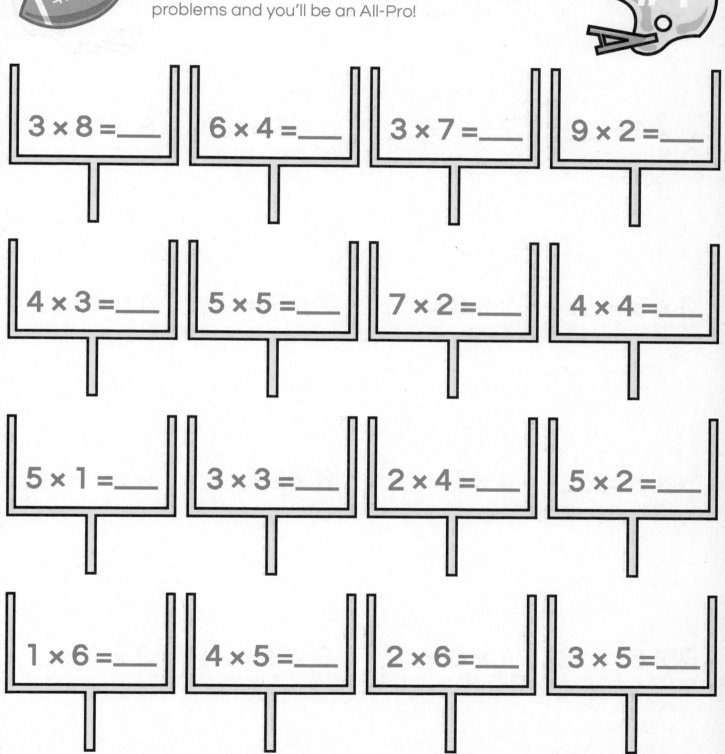

$3 \times 8 = \underline{\hspace{1cm}}$

$6 \times 4 = \underline{\hspace{1cm}}$

$3 \times 7 = \underline{\hspace{1cm}}$

$9 \times 2 = \underline{\hspace{1cm}}$

$4 \times 3 = \underline{\hspace{1cm}}$

$5 \times 5 = \underline{\hspace{1cm}}$

$7 \times 2 = \underline{\hspace{1cm}}$

$4 \times 4 = \underline{\hspace{1cm}}$

$5 \times 1 = \underline{\hspace{1cm}}$

$3 \times 3 = \underline{\hspace{1cm}}$

$2 \times 4 = \underline{\hspace{1cm}}$

$5 \times 2 = \underline{\hspace{1cm}}$

$1 \times 6 = \underline{\hspace{1cm}}$

$4 \times 5 = \underline{\hspace{1cm}}$

$2 \times 6 = \underline{\hspace{1cm}}$

$3 \times 5 = \underline{\hspace{1cm}}$

Making Multiplication Sentences

Kick off! Time to take the field and score a touchdown for the home team. Solve the following multiplication problems and you'll be an All-Pro!

6 × 4 = ___

7 × 2 = ___

3 × 5 = ___

8 × 1 = ___

3 × 3 = ___

2 × 8 = ___

7 × 3 = ___

4 × 2 = ___

8 × 3 = ___

4 × 5 = ___

6 × 2 = ___

9 × 1 = ___

7 × 8 = ___

1 × 8 = ___

9 × 3 = ___

3 × 4 = ___

Making Multiplication Sentences

Kick off! Time to take the field and score a touchdown for the home team. Solve the following multiplication problems and you'll be an All-Pro!

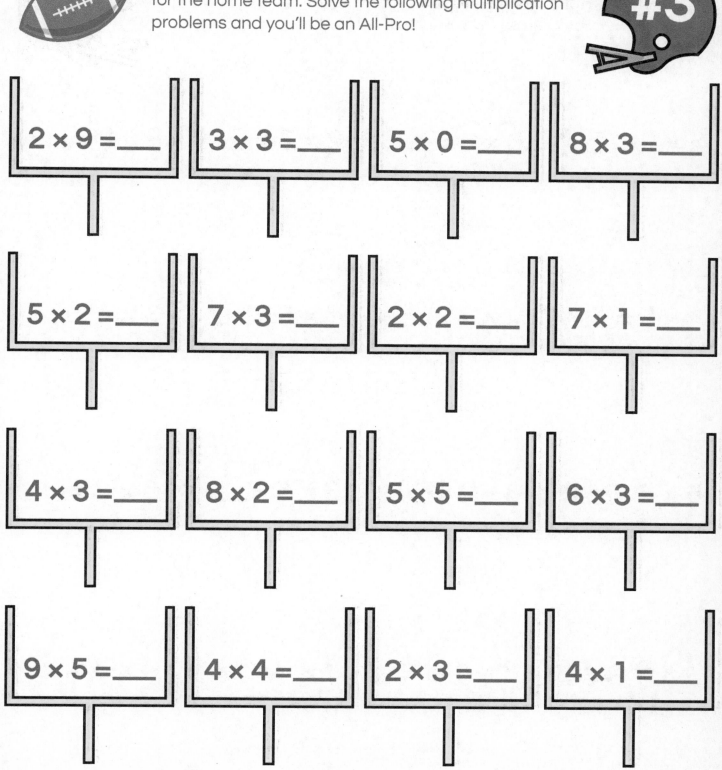

2 × 9 = ___

3 × 3 = ___

5 × 0 = ___

8 × 3 = ___

5 × 2 = ___

7 × 3 = ___

2 × 2 = ___

7 × 1 = ___

4 × 3 = ___

8 × 2 = ___

5 × 5 = ___

6 × 3 = ___

9 × 5 = ___

4 × 4 = ___

2 × 3 = ___

4 × 1 = ___

Making Multiplication Sentences

Kick off! Time to take the field and score a touchdown for the home team. Solve the following multiplication problems and you'll be an All-Pro!

#4

5 × 2 = ___   6 × 3 = ___   2 × 2 = ___   8 × 2 = ___

4 × 5 = ___   2 × 7 = ___   1 × 8 = ___   3 × 4 = ___

6 × 4 = ___   3 × 3 = ___   3 × 5 = ___   6 × 2 = ___

4 × 5 = ___   2 × 4 = ___   1 × 3 = ___   4 × 8 = ___

Making Multiplication Sentences

Kick off! Time to take the field and score a touchdown for the home team. Solve the following multiplication problems and you'll be an All-Pro!

#5

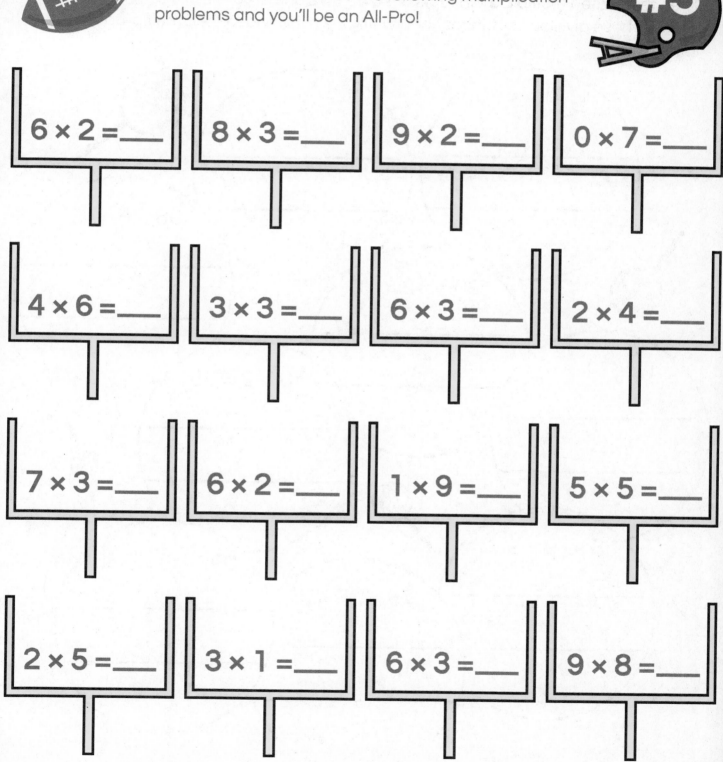

6 × 2 = ___

8 × 3 = ___

9 × 2 = ___

0 × 7 = ___

4 × 6 = ___

3 × 3 = ___

6 × 3 = ___

2 × 4 = ___

7 × 3 = ___

6 × 2 = ___

1 × 9 = ___

5 × 5 = ___

2 × 5 = ___

3 × 1 = ___

6 × 3 = ___

9 × 8 = ___

9

Find The Multiplication Facts

Multiplication is the reverse of division.

Example: If the division sentence is $12 \div 6 = 2$,

Then the related multiplication facts are $6 \times 2 = 12$ and $2 \times 6 = 12$.

Look at these division sentences, and write down the two related multiplication facts.

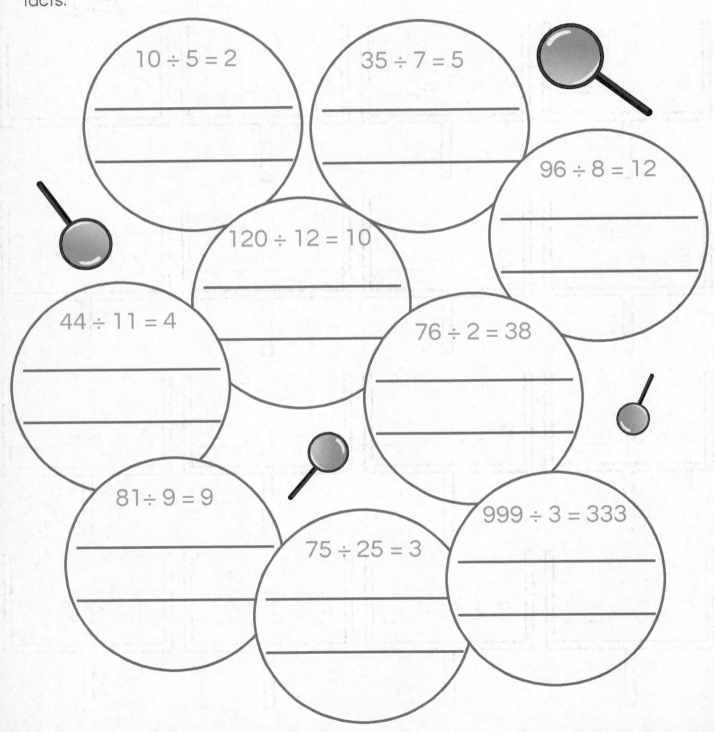

$10 \div 5 = 2$

_____

_____

$35 \div 7 = 5$

_____

_____

$96 \div 8 = 12$

_____

_____

$120 \div 12 = 10$

_____

$44 \div 11 = 4$

_____

_____

$76 \div 2 = 38$

_____

_____

$81 \div 9 = 9$

_____

_____

$75 \div 25 = 3$

_____

$999 \div 3 = 333$

_____

_____

Umbrella Math

Complete each math problem and color the page.

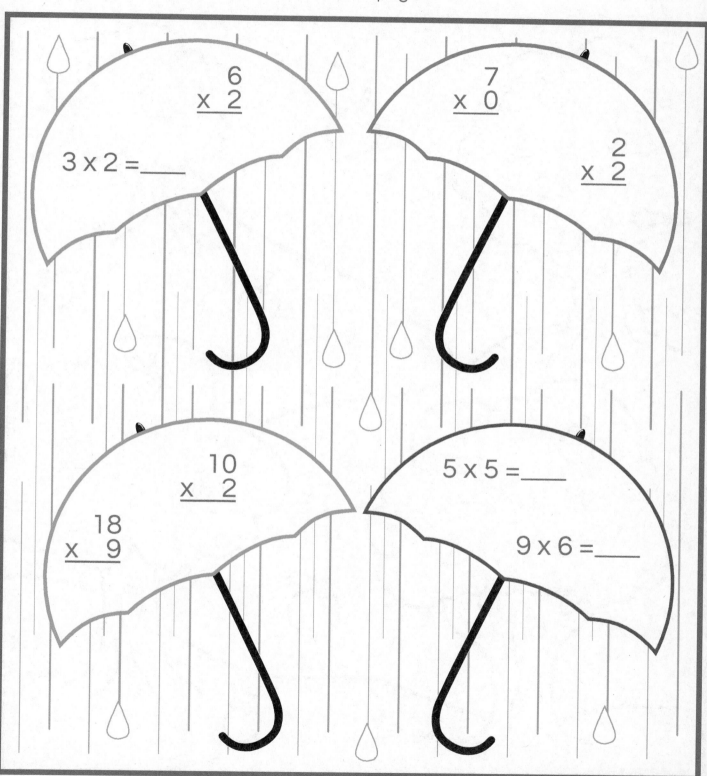

$$\begin{array}{r} 6 \\ \times\ 2 \\ \hline \end{array}$$

$3 \times 2 = \underline{}$

$$\begin{array}{r} 7 \\ \times\ 0 \\ \hline \end{array}$$

$$\begin{array}{r} 2 \\ \times\ 2 \\ \hline \end{array}$$

$$\begin{array}{r} 10 \\ \times\ 2 \\ \hline \end{array}$$

$$\begin{array}{r} 18 \\ \times\ 9 \\ \hline \end{array}$$

$5 \times 5 = \underline{}$

$9 \times 6 = \underline{}$

11

Apple Tree Math

Complete each math problem and color the page.

19
x 10

25
x 10

6
x 3

22
x 11

28
x 13

8
x 5

9
x 2

Mammoth Multiplication Problems

There is no monkeying around with these multiplication problems!

```
   72          43          28          38
 x  3        x  6        x  2        x  8
```

```
   55          19          63          78
 x  4        x  9        x  7        x  5
```

```
   49          82          57          15
 x  6        x  3        x  8        x  4
```

```
   36          67          22          89
 x  7        x  2        x  9        x  5
```

Double Digit Multiplication

They may look tough but, you can do these double digit multiplication problems!

```
    34          78          94          14
x   45      x   42      x   12      x   33
--------    --------    --------    --------
```

```
    56          84          16          65
x   77      x   24      x   51      x   11
--------    --------    --------    --------
```

```
    76          30          22          89
x   20      x   62      x   99      x   47
--------    --------    --------    --------
```

14

Greater Than Or Less Than

> "Greater Than"   < "Less Than"   = "Equal"

Directions: Solve the equations then write down the symbol that best compares each answer. Then write the answer in word form

Example:

232 x 32   **>**   22 x 150

7424   3300

Seven thousand, four hundred and twenty-four is greater than three thousand, three hundred.

1. 89   134
    x 63   x 24

_____

_____

_____

2. 346   45
    x   3   x 23

_____

_____

_____

3. 142   71
    x   10   x 20

_____

_____

_____

4. 232   560
    x   85   x 42

_____

_____

_____

5. 843   235
    x   27   x 94

_____

_____

_____

> "Greater Than"   < "Less Than"   = "Equal"

Directions: Solve the equations then write down the symbol that best compares each answer. Then write the answer in word form

Example:

232 x 32   **>**   22 x 150

7424   3300

Seven thousand, four hundred and twenty-four is greater than three thousand, three hundred.

1.   539   133
   x 223   x 624

_____

_____

_____

_____

2.   439   244
   x 173   x 324

_____

_____

_____

_____

3.   453   1223
   x 513   x 154

_____

_____

_____

_____

4.   745   394
   x 16   x 85

_____

_____

_____

_____

Multiplication Word Problems

Math isn't just for math class. It is used to solve problems in every subject. Help Mr. Hammond's class figure out their problems using math. Show your work.

Henry wants to see how many different colored crayons are in the crayon box. If there here are 4 rows of 19 crayons, how many different colors are there?

_____

Mikey is typing in the computer lab and typing at 23 words per minute. If he types for 11 minutes, how many words does he type?

_____

All of the students have a vocabulary assignment every week with 13 new words. If the school year is 40 weeks long, how many new words will they learn?

_____

Jeremy is building a toothpick skyscraper. Look at the picture below of the first floor. How many tooth picks will it take to build 12 stories? How many marshmallows will it take to build 12 stories?

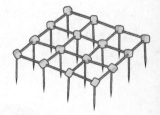

_____

It's the day before Valentine's Day and Shelley needs to get Valentine cards for all of her classmates. The desks are arranged in a rectangle 7 rows wide and 5 rows long. If there are 3 desks that are empty, how many students are in the class?

_____

Merchandise Multiplication

Use multiplication to solve the following problems. Show your work.

The Nguyen family gets movies from Movie Mail home video delivery service. They get 3 movies at the beginning of the week and return them at the end of each week. If they continue this pattern, how many movies will they see in one year? (1 year = 52 weeks)

Mr. Hayes is having friends over to watch basketball and needs to buy snacks. He buys 5 boxes of crackers. In each box there are 3 sleeves of 24 crackers. How many crackers did he buy all together? This is a two step problem. Try multiplying the numbers in different orders. Do you get the same answer?

Look at the diagram of a portion of the local grocery store's parking lot. If there are 15 rows of parking spaces in the lot like this one, how many cars can the park-ing lot fit in total?

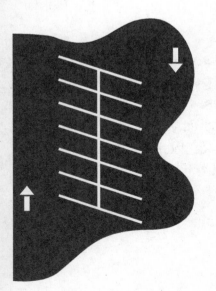

Mr. Chang is comparing television screen sizes. Screen #1 is 18 by 23 inches and screen #2 is 19 by 22 inches. Which television has the larger screen?

Wild Word Problems

Math in the animal kingdom! Use multiplication to solve the following problems. Add or subtract when necessary. Show your work.

Mario walks his dog every day. The walk path makes a giant loop that is 279 feet long. If Mario and his dog make 3 laps around the loop, how far do they walk?

Josefina's cat, Whiskers, climbed into a tree and was too scared to come down. Her dad climbed up a ladder to bring down Whiskers. If Josefina's dad had to climb up 15 ladder steps and the steps are 32 centimeters apart, how high up did Whiskers go?

Racquel buys a small aquarium for her fish collection. The fish tank is 27 inches wide, 13 inches tall, and 13 inches deep. What is the maximum volume of water can the aquarium hold? This is problem requires two multiplication steps, does the order of operations matter? Remember, Volume = Length x Width x Height.

Julie is teaching her parrot, Romeo, how to say new words. If she teaches him 11 words each month. How many words will Romeo learn in a year?

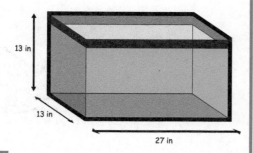

13 in

13 in

27 in

Family Vacation Multiplication

The Smiths are going on a family vacation. Use multiplication, addition, and subtraction to solve the following problems. Perform other operations as needed to help find the answers. Show your work.

Driving to the airport, the Smiths needed to fill up on gasoline. Gasoline costs 3 dollars for one gallon. If their tank holds 16 gallons, and they already have 3 gallons filled, how much money will it cost to fill the car's tank completely?

The Smiths want to visit a museum and must pay to park. They are going to be gone for 4 hours. The price of parking is as follows:

    1 Quarter = 15 minutes
    1 Dime = 5 minutes
    1 Nickel = 2 minutes

The Smiths have 8 quarters, 12 dimes and 14 nickels. Do they have enough to park for 4 hours? (Remember: 60 minutes = 1 hour)

The Smiths board the airplane to head back home. The flight attendant wants to count how many passengers are on board. Every row consists of 2, 3, and 2 seats each (see picture below). If there are 51 horizontal rows, and 13 seats are empty, how many passengers are on board?

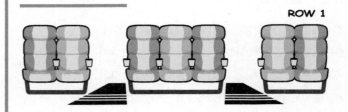

ROW 1

In total, the Smiths were flying in an airplane for 14 hours. If the airplane cruises at approximately 512 miles per hour, about how many miles did they travel all together?

Finding Factors

Factors are numbers that you multiply together to get another number.
For example, 2 multiplied by 4 equals 8. So 2 and 4 are the factors of 8. Find the factors of the numbers below. See the example.

10   = $\underline{\ 2 \times 5\ }$ 18   = $\underline{\hspace{3cm}}$

24   = $\underline{\hspace{3cm}}$ 30   = $\underline{\hspace{3cm}}$

32   = $\underline{\hspace{3cm}}$ 39   = $\underline{\hspace{3cm}}$

Find the missing factors.

15   =   3 x [   ]   21   =   3 x [   ]

45   =   9 x [   ]   42   =   7 x [   ]

---

36   =   2 x 2 x 3 x [   ]

60   =   2 x 3 x 2 x [   ]

75   =   5 x 3 x [   ]

* When the factor is a prime number, it is called a prime factor.

21

Multiply Three Numbers

Here's a trick! First, multiply the first number by the second one. Then multiply the product of the first two numbers by the third number. Find the product of these multiplication sentences. The first one is done for you.

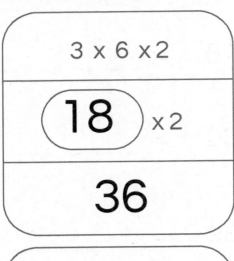

3 x 6 x 2

(18) x 2

36

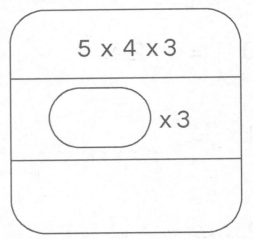

5 x 4 x 3

( ) x 3

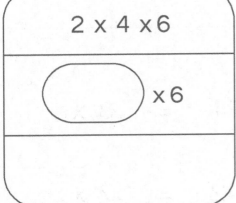

2 x 4 x 6

( ) x 6

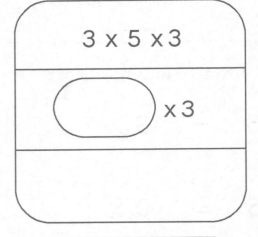

3 x 5 x 3

( ) x 3

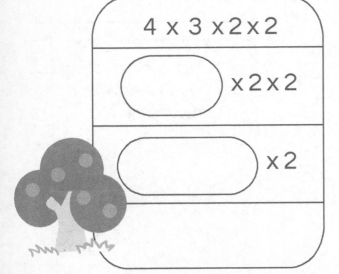

4 x 3 x 2 x 2

( ) x 2 x 2

( ) x 2

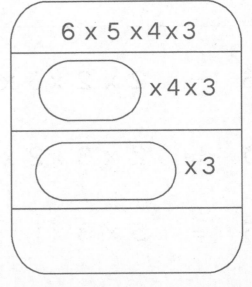

6 x 5 x 4 x 3

( ) x 4 x 3

( ) x 3

Math-Go-Round

Multiplication | Difficulty: ★★★

Find a friend and practice your multiplication skills. Find two coins or game pieces and place them on the square labeled START. Choose one of the problems to solve and move your game piece clockwise around the board to that problem's answer. Keep track of the number of corners you go around on each move. For each one, give yourself a point. The player with the most points at the end is the winner. Keep score with the table below.

Game Board

+1 Point

Square values (top row)
1,610	3,021	8,840	8,772

+1 Point

Left column (top to bottom): 6,384 — 4,462 — 3,861 — 7,957

Right column (top to bottom): 1,419 — 9,322 — 8,631 — 3,336

Bottom row: 1,694 — 2,916 — 4,653 — 9,860

START

+1 Point

+1 Point

Problems

$$137 \times 63$$
$$104 \times 85$$
$$141 \times 33$$
$$115 \times 14$$
$$158 \times 59$$
$$159 \times 19$$
$$152 \times 42$$
$$194 \times 23$$
$$170 \times 58$$
$$109 \times 73$$
$$143 \times 27$$
$$172 \times 51$$
$$154 \times 11$$
$$129 \times 11$$

Score Table

	Player 1	Player 2
Round 1		
Round 2		
Round 3		
Round 4		
Round 5		
Round 6		
Round 7		
Round 8		
Total		

Great job!

is an Education.com math superstar

Fun
with
Fractions

Odd One Out: Practicing Fractions

In each line there is one shape whose value is not equal to the others. Color it in.

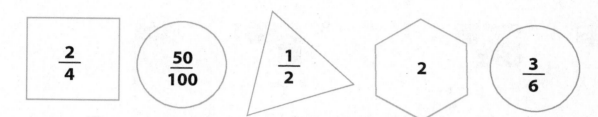

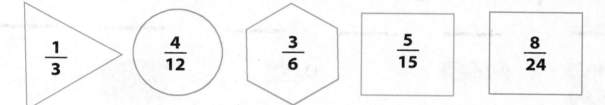

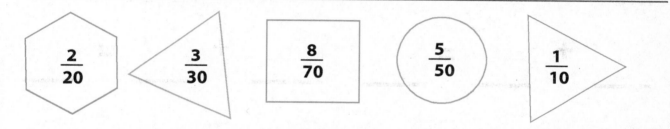

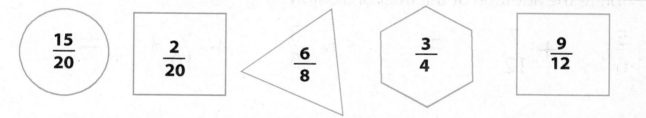

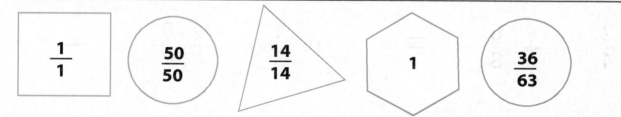

Fraction Addition

Write the fraction of the colored boxes in the space provided and then add the fractions together.

A.

$$\underline{} + \underline{} = \underline{}$$

B.

$$\underline{} + \underline{} = \underline{}$$

C.

$$\underline{} + \underline{} = \underline{}$$

D.

$$\underline{} + \underline{} = \underline{}$$

Complete the addition of the fractions below.

E. $\dfrac{5}{6} + \dfrac{7}{12} =$ F. $\dfrac{3}{5} + \dfrac{4}{10} =$

G. $\dfrac{2}{4} + \dfrac{6}{8} =$ H. $\dfrac{1}{3} + \dfrac{8}{9} =$

I. $\dfrac{3}{4} + \dfrac{5}{6} =$ J. $\dfrac{2}{3} + \dfrac{4}{5} =$

Simple Sherwin's
Simple Fractions

Simple Sherwin likes everything around him to be neat and simple. Help him rewrite these fractions in their most simplified form.

Example:

$$\frac{4}{12} = \frac{1}{3}$$

$$\frac{4}{12} \begin{array}{c} \div 4 \\ \div 4 \end{array} = \frac{1}{3}$$

$\dfrac{4}{6} =$ _____ $\dfrac{2}{10} =$ _____ $\dfrac{21}{28} =$ _____ $\dfrac{10}{15} =$ _____ $\dfrac{6}{18} =$ _____

$\dfrac{4}{8} =$ _____ $\dfrac{16}{20} =$ _____ $\dfrac{7}{14} =$ _____ $\dfrac{6}{15} =$ _____ $\dfrac{12}{20} =$ _____

31

Simple Sylvia's
Simple Fractions

Simple Sylvia likes everything around her to be neat and simple. Help her rewrite these fractions in their most simplified form.

Example:

$$\frac{12}{15} = \frac{4}{5}$$

$$\frac{12 \div 3}{15 \div 3} = \frac{4}{5}$$

$\dfrac{2}{8} = $ —— $\dfrac{10}{15} = $ —— $\dfrac{6}{12} = $ —— $\dfrac{21}{28} = $ —— $\dfrac{3}{6} = $ ——

$\dfrac{5}{15} = $ —— $\dfrac{8}{20} = $ —— $\dfrac{3}{12} = $ —— $\dfrac{2}{10} = $ —— $\dfrac{14}{21} = $ ——

Simple Scooter's Simple Fractions

Simple Scooter likes everything around him to be neat and simple. Help him rewrite these fractions in their most simplified form.

Example:

$$\frac{10}{15} = \frac{2}{3}$$

$$\frac{10 \div 5}{15 \div 5} = \frac{2}{3}$$

$$\frac{12}{16} = \underline{\quad} \qquad \frac{3}{15} = \underline{\quad} \qquad \frac{8}{10} = \underline{\quad} \qquad \frac{2}{4} = \underline{\quad} \qquad \frac{18}{24} = \underline{\quad}$$

$$\frac{14}{21} = \underline{\quad} \qquad \frac{4}{16} = \underline{\quad} \qquad \frac{6}{9} = \underline{\quad} \qquad \frac{7}{28} = \underline{\quad} \qquad \frac{20}{25} = \underline{\quad}$$

33

MATH
FRACTIONS

Steer & Simplify #1

Navigate the treacherous seas by simplifying the following fractions. Use the compass on the right to guide you. Start at the red arrow and go north, south, east or west to the next square with each fraction your reduce. Draw a line to track your journey. Show your work.

Compass Instructions: Once you reduce a fraction completely, look at its denominator and then find that number on the compass and move in the direction it points.

$$\frac{9}{54} = \underline{\quad}$$

$$\frac{6}{15} = \underline{\quad}$$

$$\frac{6}{8} = \underline{\quad}$$

$$\frac{27}{45} = \underline{\quad}$$

$$\frac{16}{24} = \underline{\quad}$$

$$\frac{24}{27} = \underline{\quad}$$

$$\frac{35}{84} = \underline{\quad}$$

$$\frac{18}{60} = \underline{\quad}$$

$$\frac{15}{30} = \underline{\quad}$$

$$\frac{5}{40} = \underline{\quad}$$

$$\frac{32}{40} = \underline{\quad}$$

$$\frac{4}{6} = \underline{\quad}$$

11 is between 9 and 12, so go west

$$\frac{9}{18} = \underline{\quad}$$

$$\frac{28}{40} = \underline{\quad}$$

$$\frac{9}{27} = \underline{\quad}$$

$$\frac{40}{55} = \frac{8}{11}$$

Steer & Simplify #2

Navigate the treacherous seas by simplifying the following fractions. Use the compass on the right to guide you. Start at the red arrow and go north, south, east or west to the next square with each fraction your reduce. Draw a line to track your journey. Show your work.

Compass Instructions: Once you reduce a fraction completely, look at its <u>denominator</u> and then find that number on the compass and move in the direction it points.

$$\frac{15}{40} = \underline{\quad} \qquad \frac{27}{90} = \underline{\quad} \qquad \frac{5}{60} = \underline{\quad} \qquad \frac{12}{42} \begin{smallmatrix} \div 6 \\ \div 6 \end{smallmatrix} = \frac{2}{7}$$

$$\frac{12}{30} = \underline{\quad} \qquad \frac{27}{72} = \underline{\quad} \qquad \frac{8}{16} = \underline{\quad} \qquad \frac{7}{63} = \underline{\quad}$$

$$\frac{2}{16} = \underline{\quad} \qquad \frac{30}{55} = \underline{\quad} \qquad \frac{7}{14} = \underline{\quad} \qquad \frac{15}{24} = \underline{\quad}$$

$$\frac{11}{55} = \underline{\quad} \qquad \frac{12}{54} = \underline{\quad} \qquad \frac{8}{12} = \underline{\quad} \qquad \frac{49}{70} = \underline{\quad}$$

Steer & Simplify #3

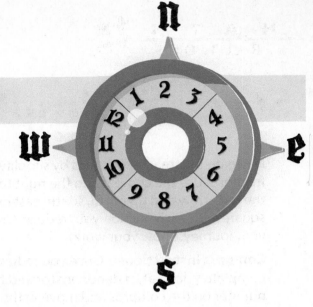

Navigate the treacherous seas by simplifying the following fractions. Use the compass on the right to guide you. Start at the red arrow and go north, south, east or west to the next square with each fraction your reduce. Draw a line to track your journey. Show your work.

Compass Instructions: Once you reduce a fraction completely, look at its <u>denominator</u> and then find that number on the compass and move in the direction it points.

$$\frac{4}{20} = \underline{\quad}$$ $$\frac{6}{36} = \underline{\quad}$$ $$\frac{18}{45} = \underline{\quad}$$ $$\frac{7}{49} = \underline{\quad}$$

$$\frac{4}{6} = \underline{\quad}$$ $$\frac{10}{14} = \underline{\quad}$$ $$\frac{27}{90} = \underline{\quad}$$ $$\frac{25}{55} = \underline{\quad}$$

$$\frac{3}{9} = \underline{\quad}$$ $$\frac{24}{27} = \underline{\quad}$$ $$\frac{20}{25} = \underline{\quad}$$ $$\frac{15}{21} = \underline{\quad}$$

$$\frac{10}{15} \begin{smallmatrix} \div\,5 \\ \div\,5 \end{smallmatrix} = \frac{2}{\underline{3}}$$ $$\frac{9}{45} = \underline{\quad}$$ $$\frac{4}{8} = \underline{\quad}$$ $$\frac{35}{45} = \underline{\quad}$$

36

Steer & Simplify #4

Navigate the treacherous seas by simplifying the following fractions. Use the compass on the right to guide you. Start at the red arrow and go north, south, east or west to the next square with each fraction your reduce. Draw a line to track your journey. Show your work.

Compass Instructions: Once you reduce a fraction completely, look at its de<u>nominator</u> and then find that number on the compass and move in the direction it points.

$\dfrac{6}{15} = \underline{\quad}$ $\dfrac{5}{35} = \underline{\quad}$ $\dfrac{4}{40} = \underline{\quad}$ $\dfrac{4}{48} = \underline{\quad}$

$\dfrac{8}{40} = \underline{\quad}$ $\dfrac{15}{33} = \underline{\quad}$ $\dfrac{5}{30} = \underline{\quad}$ $\dfrac{7}{21} = \underline{\quad}$

$\dfrac{2}{8} = \underline{\quad}$ $\dfrac{9}{12} = \underline{\quad}$ $\dfrac{3}{6} = \underline{\quad}$ $\dfrac{28}{32} \genfrac{}{}{0pt}{}{\div 4}{\div 4} = \dfrac{7}{8}$

$\dfrac{5}{10} = \underline{\quad}$ $\dfrac{18}{66} = \underline{\quad}$ $\dfrac{42}{60} = \underline{\quad}$ $\dfrac{2}{24} = \underline{\quad}$

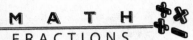
Skill Practice #1
Simplifying Fractions

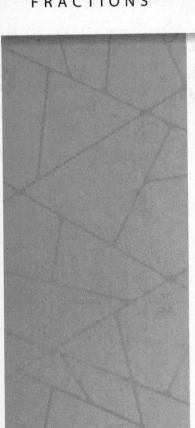

❋ Simplify the following fractions. Show your work.

$$\frac{15}{30} \begin{smallmatrix} \div 15 \\ = \\ \div 15 \end{smallmatrix} \frac{1}{2} \qquad\qquad \frac{16}{80} = \underline{\quad} \qquad\qquad \frac{18}{24} = \underline{\quad}$$

$$\frac{45}{54} = \underline{\quad} \qquad\qquad \frac{55}{66} = \underline{\quad} \qquad\qquad \frac{18}{72} = \underline{\quad}$$

$$\frac{14}{42} = \underline{\quad} \qquad\qquad \frac{27}{54} = \underline{\quad} \qquad\qquad \frac{35}{50} = \underline{\quad}$$

❋ Now that you've got the hang of it, look closely at the following fractions. They do not simplify very well, but they are very close to a simplifiable fraction. For example, **19/60** cannot be simplified, but we know that **20/60 = 1/3**. So, **19/60** can be approximated to **1/3**. Be sure to show your work.

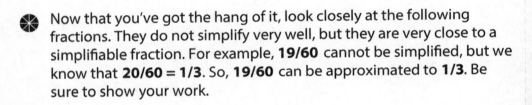

$$\frac{19}{30} \approx \frac{2}{3} \qquad\qquad \frac{14}{41} \approx \underline{\quad} \qquad\qquad \frac{20}{81} \approx \underline{\quad}$$

$$\approx \frac{20}{30} \begin{smallmatrix} \div 10 \\ \div 10 \end{smallmatrix} \rightarrow \frac{2}{3}$$

$$\frac{24}{49} \approx \underline{\quad} \qquad\qquad \frac{17}{80} \approx \underline{\quad} \qquad\qquad \frac{27}{37} \approx \underline{\quad}$$

$$\frac{23}{72} \approx \underline{\quad} \qquad\qquad \frac{13}{21} \approx \underline{\quad} \qquad\qquad \frac{99}{100} \approx \underline{\quad}$$

Skill Practice #2
Simplifying Fractions

✸ Simplify the following fractions. Show your work.

$$\frac{22}{66} \begin{smallmatrix} \div 22 \\ = \\ \div 22 \end{smallmatrix} \frac{1}{3} \qquad \frac{15}{20} = \underline{\quad} \qquad \frac{28}{42} = \underline{\quad}$$

$$\frac{12}{36} = \underline{\quad} \qquad \frac{28}{35} = \underline{\quad} \qquad \frac{24}{40} = \underline{\quad}$$

$$\frac{19}{76} = \underline{\quad} \qquad \frac{18}{60} = \underline{\quad} \qquad \frac{23}{46} = \underline{\quad}$$

✸ Now that you've got the hang of it, look closely at the following fractions. They do not simplify very well, but they are very close to a simplifiable fraction. For example, **45/61** cannot be simplified, but we know that **45/60 = 3/4**. So, **45/61** can be approximated to **3/4**. Be sure to show your work.

$$\frac{45}{51} \approx \frac{9}{10} \qquad \frac{11}{45} \approx \underline{\quad} \qquad \frac{13}{24} \approx \underline{\quad}$$

$$\approx \frac{45 \div 5}{50 \div 5} \rightarrow \frac{9}{10}$$

$$\frac{23}{30} \approx \underline{\quad} \qquad \frac{89}{90} \approx \underline{\quad} \qquad \frac{31}{36} \approx \underline{\quad}$$

$$\frac{37}{72} \approx \underline{\quad} \qquad \frac{49}{64} \approx \underline{\quad} \qquad \frac{10}{61} \approx \underline{\quad}$$

M A T H
F R A C T I O N S
Skill Practice #3
Simplifying Fractions

Simplify the following fractions. Show your work.

$$\frac{12}{30} \begin{matrix} \div 6 \\ \div 6 \end{matrix} = \frac{2}{5} \qquad\qquad \frac{20}{24} = \underline{\quad\quad} \qquad\qquad \frac{63}{70} = \underline{\quad\quad}$$

$$\frac{5}{15} = \underline{\quad\quad} \qquad\qquad \frac{27}{45} = \underline{\quad\quad} \qquad\qquad \frac{10}{20} = \underline{\quad\quad}$$

$$\frac{3}{18} = \underline{\quad\quad} \qquad\qquad \frac{18}{27} = \underline{\quad\quad} \qquad\qquad \frac{24}{32} = \underline{\quad\quad}$$

Now that you've got the hang of it, look closely at the following fractions. They do not simplify very well, but they are very close to a simplifiable fraction. For example, **51/100** cannot be simplified, but we know that **50/100 = 1/2**. So, **50/100** can be approximated to **1/2**. Be sure to show your work.

$$\frac{16}{63} \approx \frac{1}{4} \qquad\qquad \frac{75}{99} \approx \underline{\quad\quad} \qquad\qquad \frac{13}{25} \approx \underline{\quad\quad}$$

$$\approx \frac{16}{64} \begin{matrix} \div 16 \\ \div 16 \end{matrix} \rightarrow \frac{1}{4}$$

$$\frac{19}{100} \approx \underline{\quad\quad} \qquad\qquad \frac{11}{72} \approx \underline{\quad\quad} \qquad\qquad \frac{41}{63} \approx \underline{\quad\quad}$$

$$\frac{28}{71} \approx \underline{\quad\quad} \qquad\qquad \frac{24}{99} \approx \underline{\quad\quad} \qquad\qquad \frac{19}{98} \approx \underline{\quad\quad}$$

Feed the Kramsters #1

Kramsters are very picky eaters. Feed each kramster the correct number of pellets by converting the following improper fractions to mixed numbers. Color in the pellets to match each mixed number.

EXAMPLE:

$\dfrac{13}{4}$

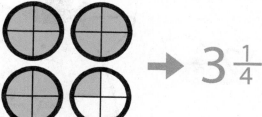

$\rightarrow$ $3\frac{1}{4}$

$\dfrac{12}{6}$

$\dfrac{15}{4}$

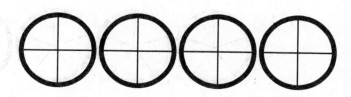 

$\dfrac{3}{2}$

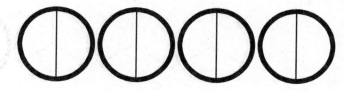 

$\dfrac{14}{5}$

For the last one, shade in the pellets without guidelines.

$\dfrac{20}{6}$

Feed the Kramsters #2

Kramsters are very picky eaters. Feed each kramster the correct number of pellets by converting the following improper fractions to mixed numbers. Color in the pellets to match each mixed number.

EXAMPLE:

$\dfrac{8}{3}$

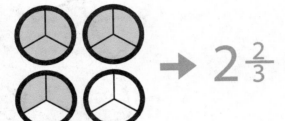 $\rightarrow 2\dfrac{2}{3}$

$\dfrac{16}{4}$

$\dfrac{13}{5}$

$\dfrac{9}{3}$

$\dfrac{12}{5}$

For the last one, shade in the pellets using your own outlines.

$\dfrac{7}{2}$

42

Feed the Kramsters #3

Kramsters are very picky eaters. Feed each kramster the correct number of pellets by converting the following improper fractions to mixed numbers. Color in the pellets to match each mixed number.

EXAMPLE:

$\dfrac{9}{4}$ 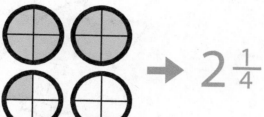 → $2\dfrac{1}{4}$

$\dfrac{9}{5}$

$\dfrac{3}{2}$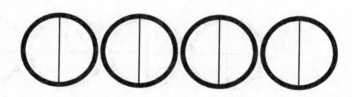

$\dfrac{10}{3}$

$\dfrac{6}{4}$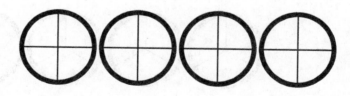

For the last one, shade in the pellets using your own outlines.

$\dfrac{16}{5}$

43

Feed the Kramsters #4

Kramsters are very picky eaters. Feed each kramster the correct number of pellets by converting the following improper fractions to mixed numbers. Color in the pellets to match each mixed number.

EXAMPLE:

$\dfrac{7}{2}$

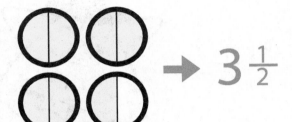

$\dfrac{5}{2}$

$\dfrac{12}{4}$

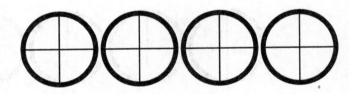

$\dfrac{11}{5}$

$\dfrac{11}{3}$

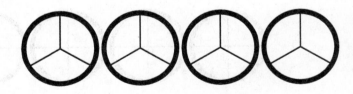

For the last one, shade in the pellets using your own outlines.

$\dfrac{10}{4}$

44

Feed the Kramsters #5

Kramsters are very picky eaters. Feed each kramster the correct number of pellets by converting the following improper fractions to mixed numbers. Color in the pellets to match each mixed number.

EXAMPLE:

$\dfrac{12}{5}$ 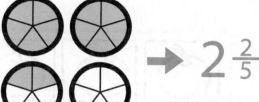 $\rightarrow 2\dfrac{2}{5}$

$\dfrac{6}{3}$

$\dfrac{7}{4}$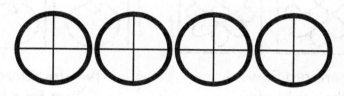

$\dfrac{8}{2}$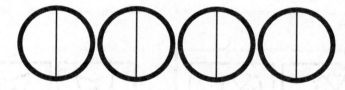

$\dfrac{11}{5}$

For the last one, shade in the pellets using your own outlines.

$\dfrac{9}{4}$

45

Colorful Plants: Practicing Fractions

Color in the flowers and fruits according to the description below.

One-third are red flowers.
Two-sixths are in pink.
Three-ninths are in blue.

Two-fourths of the apples are green.
Two-fourths of the rest are red.
What is left are black.

Half of the tulips are orange.
One-sixth are in pink.
The rest are red.

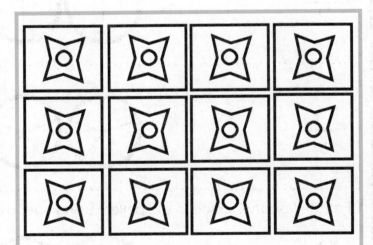

One-third are red flowers.
One-fourth are in pink.
The rest are in purple.

Ranking Fractions

Rank the fractions in order from the largest to the smallest value and write the order in the space below. **Bonus: Find the row that has two equivalent fractions.**

$\frac{1}{5}$	$\frac{3}{4}$	$\frac{1}{3}$	$\frac{2}{4}$	$\frac{6}{24}$

$\frac{1}{1}$	$\frac{12}{30}$	$\frac{3}{30}$	$\frac{8}{24}$	$\frac{4}{10}$

$\frac{5}{8}$	$\frac{5}{15}$	$\frac{15}{20}$	$\frac{14}{14}$	$\frac{3}{6}$

$\frac{3}{6}$	$\frac{50}{50}$	$\frac{9}{12}$	$\frac{2}{20}$	$\frac{7}{10}$

1	$\frac{50}{100}$	2	$\frac{4}{10}$	$\frac{2}{3}$

$\frac{1}{2}$	$\frac{1}{3}$	$\frac{3}{4}$	$\frac{4}{5}$	$\frac{5}{6}$

Great job!

is an Education.com math superstar

Learn
Fractions
and
Decimals

Skill Practice
Rounding and Place Values

For the decimals given, write out the name of the number's last place value.

4.25<u>3</u>	12.02	95.408
thousandths		

0.021	10.5	8.506

8.52	9.321	50.2

89.8	4,512.3	88.22

For the decimals given, round off each number to the place value listed above its row. In the last row, round off to the underlined place value.

Tenths

8.231	45.128	0.981	2.012	16.061
8.2				

Hundredths

8.2561	66.2135	0.8646	7.9843	52.1143
8.26				

Thousandths

0.8643	6.5127	0.2155	7.4541	1.8950
0.864				

Mixed

45.<u>1</u>952	0.23<u>1</u>5	81.00<u>5</u>3	90.<u>5</u>50	0.01<u>8</u>6
45.20				

53

Skill Practice 2
Rounding and Place Values

For the decimals given, write out the name of the number's last place value

90.<u>3</u>	1.57	8.6
tenths		
19.521	325.40	20.050
34.8	18.629	4.51
99.016	16.52	7.1

For the decimals given, round off each number to the place value listed above its row. In the last row, round off to the underlined place value.

Tenths

5.291	51.0526	4.832	65.247	1.366
5.3				

Hundredths

8.2952	21.5061	84.9315	14.6147	8.4473
8.30				

Thousandths

52.3615	0.2381	12.4534	9.0267	9.4125
52.362				

Mixed

11.24<u>5</u>3	25.<u>8</u>963	94.4135	6.3<u>5</u>19	5.<u>7</u>082
11.245				

Skill Practice
Addition with Decimals

Solve the following addition problems by rewriting each expression vertically and solving. Remember to line up the decimal places when writing the problem vertically.

16.2 + 9.05

$$\begin{array}{r} 16.20 \\ + 9.05 \\ \hline 25.25 \end{array}$$

2.513 + 19.61

24.9 + 5.73

72.52 + 0.214

2.83 + 1.994

243.1 + 3.07

1.203 + 16.48

14.63 + 12.9

10.5 + 3.481

37.53 + 22.8

1.358 + 250.2

0.53 + 64.095

55

Sheep Math

Complete each math problem and color the page!

9.4
+ 1.8

7.3
+ 5.8

3.7
+ 5.5

5.7
+ 4.9

7.3
+ 1.9

Skill Practice

Subtracting with Decimals

Solve the following subtraction problems by rewriting each expression vertically and solving. Remember to line up the decimal places when writing the problem vertically.

| 95.2 - 5.58 | 8.23 - 1.257 | 61.3 - 7.35 |

```
   95.20
 -  5.58
   89.62
```

| 10.08 - 9.6 | 7.109 - 3.3 | 75.3 - 13.19 |

| 8.024 - 6.76 | 18.8 - 14.52 | 5.6 - 2.863 |

| 7.25 - 6.01 | 25.3 - 4.192 | 70.5 - 4.61 |

Skill Practice **2**

Subtracting with Decimals

Solve the following subtraction problems by rewriting each expression vertically and solving. Remember to line up the decimal places when writing the problem vertically.

18.63 - 2.041

$$
\begin{array}{r}
18.630 \\
- 2.041 \\
\hline
16.589
\end{array}
$$

8.45 - 6.3

7.41 - 0.196

4.215 - 3.2

20.12 - 13.7

4.2 - 0.429

126.4 - 0.147

77.98 - 15.6

43.2 - 12.75

9.35 - 3.282

62.45 - 3.187

1.248 - 1.19

Conversation:
Practice Ordering Decimals

Order the decimal numbers on the conversation bubbles from largest to smallest, then use the letters to answer the question below.

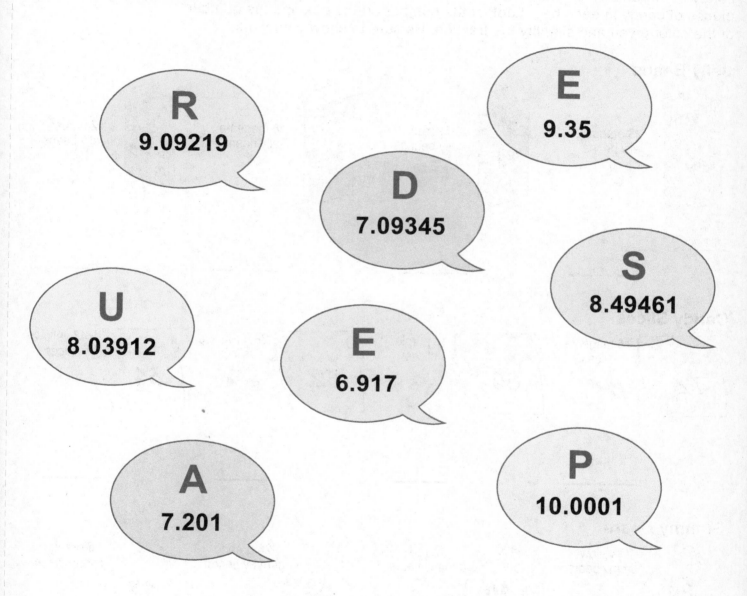

R 9.09219

E 9.35

D 7.09345

U 8.03912

E 6.917

S 8.49461

A 7.201

P 10.0001

Jacob is trying to

___ ___ ___ ___ ___ ___ ___ ___ **Jack.**

Fractions:

Fractions are everywhere, even in candy! Look at the boxes of candy below and simplify the ratios of the colors to the total number of pieces of candy in each bag. Look at the number on the box and the number of the color given and simplify the fraction. Be sure to show your work.

Jelly Beans

 **18** orange jelly beans

 **21** blue jelly beans

 **18** magenta jelly beans

 **24** green jelly beans

$$\frac{\text{orange jelly beans}}{\text{total \#}} = \frac{18 \div 9}{45 \div 9} = \frac{2}{5}$$

Candy Slices

 **45** magenta slices

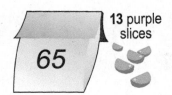 **13** purple slices

 **26** turquoise slices

 **48** yellow slices

Gummy Bears

 **21** yellow gummy bears

 **12** red gummy bears

 **26** green gummy bears

 **5** orange gummy bears

Activity: With your own favorite colorful candy, find the fractions of each color in the bag

Fraction Action!
Writing The Lowest Form: Take 1

To reduce a fraction, first find the common factor of the numerator and the denominator.

The numerator $\longrightarrow$ $\dfrac{6}{9}$
The denominator $\longrightarrow$

The common factor of 6 and 9 is 3 because $6 = 2 \times 3$ and $9 = 3 \times 3$
Then, divide the numerator and denominator by 3.

divide the numerator $\longrightarrow$ $\dfrac{6 \div 3}{9 \div 3}$
divide the denominator $\longrightarrow$

Therefore, the reduced form of $\dfrac{6}{9}$ is $\dfrac{2}{3}$.

Find the lowest form of the fractions below. Write it down. Show your work.

$\dfrac{4}{12}$

$\dfrac{5}{30}$

$\dfrac{8}{24}$

Fill in the missing numerator or denominator.

$\dfrac{7}{35} = \dfrac{1}{\underline{}}$ 　　　　 $\dfrac{3}{63} = \dfrac{1}{\underline{}}$

$\dfrac{6}{36} = \dfrac{}{6}$ 　　　　 $\dfrac{9}{33} = \dfrac{3}{\underline{}}$

Fraction Action!
Writing The Lowest Form: Take 2

To reduce a fraction, first find the common factor of the numerator and the denominator.

The numerator $\longrightarrow$ $\dfrac{8}{12}$
The denominator $\longrightarrow$

The common factor of 8 and 12 is 4 because $8 = 2 \times 4$ and $12 = 3 \times 4$.

Then, divide the numerator and denominator by 4.

divide the numerator $\longrightarrow$ $\dfrac{8 \div 4}{12 \div 4}$
divide the denominator $\longrightarrow$

Therefore, the reduced form of $\dfrac{8}{12}$ is $\dfrac{2}{3}$.

Look at the shading area on the left side. Write the fraction and then reduce it to the lowest form.

$= \quad \dfrac{2}{4} \quad = \quad \dfrac{1}{2}$

$= \quad \underline{\quad} \quad = \quad \underline{\quad}$

$= \quad \underline{\quad} \quad = \quad \underline{\quad}$

Find the lowest form of the fraction below. Write it down. Show your work.

$\dfrac{8}{36}$

$\dfrac{6}{39}$

The Greatest and The Least: Practicing Fractions

Color in the shape with the greatest value red, and the shape with the least value blue.

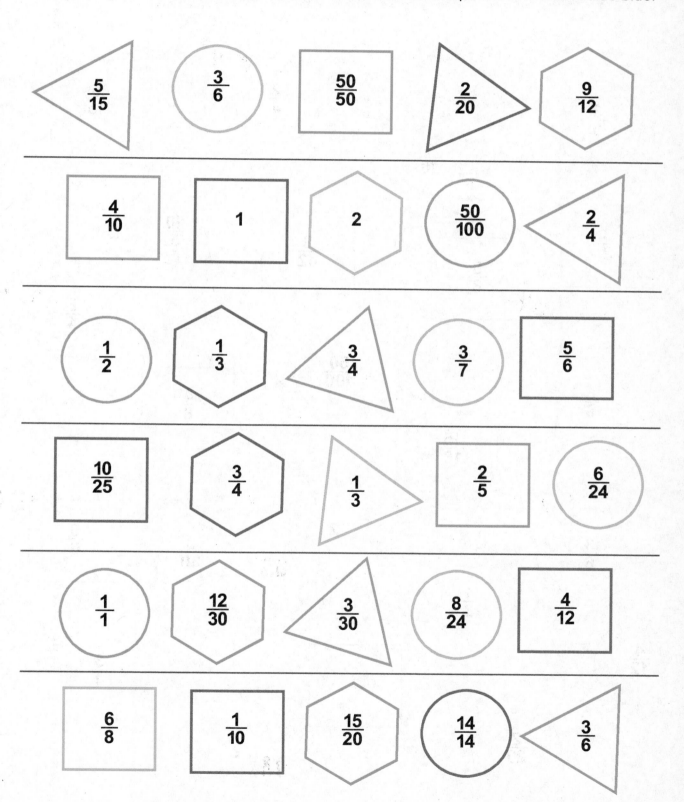

Colorful Shapes: Practicing Fractions

Color in the shapes that have the same value with the same color.

Introduction to Integers

Fill in the missing numbers to complete the number line.

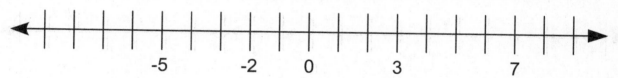

-5   -2   0   3   7

Fill in the blanks with neutral, positive or negative.

Zero is a _____ integer.

A whole number less than zero is a _____ integer.

A whole number greater than zero is a _____ integer.

Whole numbers that are _____ integers can be written with or without a sign.

Circle the integers

-4   ½   3   -2   0   ¾   +6   8   -7   ¼   1   +9

Match the opposite integers.

3   5   2   4   1   6   7

-5   -2   -3   -6   -7   -4   -1

Adding Integers

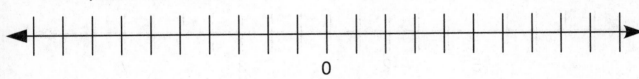

Complete the number line.

```
◄──┼──┼──┼──┼──┼──┼──┼──┼──┼──┼──┼──┼──┼──┼──┼──┼──┼──┼──┼──┼──►
                                    0
```

Complete the addition problems.

-2	+4	+5	-6	+8	-1	-9
+ +3	+ -2	+ -1	+ +2	+ +2	+ -5	+ +8

+7	-3	-4	+9	+6	-5	-4
+ +3	+ +6	+ +5	+ -7	+ -7	+ +6	+ -3

Complete the word problems. Use the table to help you.

The temperature is 5 degrees below zero.
The temperature falls 15 degrees.
What is the temperature now?

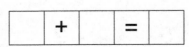

A seed is planted 2 inches below the ground.
The plant grows 6 inches from the seed.
How tall is the plant above the ground?

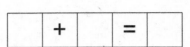

The base of a hill is 11 feet below sea level.
The hill is 27 feet high.
How much of the hill is above sea level?

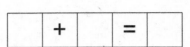

Great job!

is an Education.com math superstar

Operations
Practice

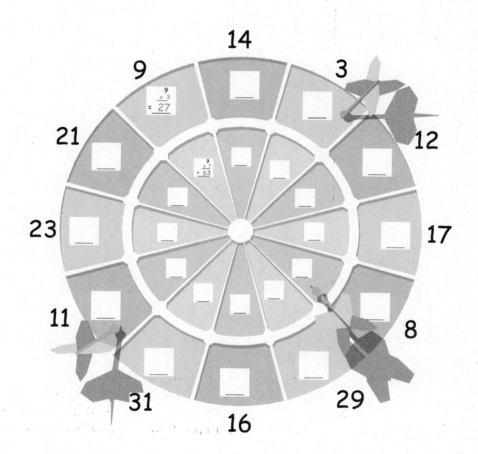

RIDDLE ME MATH!

Directions: Solve each math problem. Then find the answer and write the letter in the correct place to solve the riddles.

WHAT CAN YOU CATCH AND NOT THROW? A $\underline{C}$ $\underline{}$ $\underline{}$ $\underline{}$.
1   2   3   4

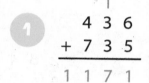

```
      1
 1    4 3 6        2    2 0 4        3    8 2 5        4    1 6 3
    + 7 3 5           + 5 9 6           + 4 8 1           + 8 3 0
    ---------
    1 1 7 1
```

WHAT KIND OF COAT CAN ONLY BE PUT ON WHEN WET? A $\underline{}$ $\underline{}$ $\underline{}$
5   6   7

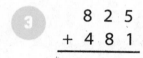

$\underline{}$ $\underline{}$ $\underline{}$ $\underline{}$ $\underline{}$ $\underline{}$ $\underline{}$ $\underline{}$.
8   9 10 11 12 13 14 15

```
 5    6 7 3        6    7 4 8        7    1 1 9        8    4 8 5
    + 3 4 9           + 6 9 7           + 2 5 0           + 2 1 5

 9    7 2 9       10    8 7 6       11    9 0 3       12    8 3 6
    + 1 6 4           + 5 3 3           + 2 0 3           + 7 2 0

13    5 8 5       14    9 5 8       15    3 3 3
    + 4 9 9           + 2 4 7           + 1 3 8
```

A. 369   F. 1409   T. 471   D. 993   O. 800   C. 1022   A. 1556   O. 1445

O. 893   P. 1106   ~~C. 1171~~   N. 1205   I. 1084   T. 700   L. 1306

RIDDLE ME MATH!

Directions: Solve each math problem. Then find the answer and write the letter in the correct place to solve the riddles.

WHAT CAN FILL A ROOM BUT TAKES UP NO SPACE? L __ __ __ __ .
1   2   3   4   5

1.
$$\begin{array}{r} 5\ 13 \\ 6\ \cancel{4}\ 10 \\ -\ 2\ 6\ 4 \\ \hline 3\ 7\ 6 \end{array}$$

2.
$$\begin{array}{r} 8\ 2\ 9 \\ -\ 1\ 0\ 0 \\ \hline \end{array}$$

3.
$$\begin{array}{r} 4\ 5\ 5 \\ -\ 2\ 8\ 3 \\ \hline \end{array}$$

4.
$$\begin{array}{r} 9\ 8\ 8 \\ -\ 5\ 2\ 7 \\ \hline \end{array}$$

5.
$$\begin{array}{r} 2\ 8\ 4 \\ -\ 2\ 5\ 9 \\ \hline \end{array}$$

WHAT HAS A FOOT ON EACH SIDE AND ONE IN THE MIDDLE?

__ __ __ __ __ __ __ __ __ .
6 7 8 9 10 11 12 13 14

6.
$$\begin{array}{r} 7\ 2\ 2 \\ -\ 3\ 4\ 6 \\ \hline \end{array}$$

7.
$$\begin{array}{r} 8\ 2\ 6 \\ -\ 4\ 6\ 5 \\ \hline \end{array}$$

8.
$$\begin{array}{r} 5\ 6\ 3 \\ -\ 3\ 7\ 2 \\ \hline \end{array}$$

9.
$$\begin{array}{r} 2\ 7\ 8 \\ -\ 1\ 3\ 4 \\ \hline \end{array}$$

10.
$$\begin{array}{r} 8\ 5\ 4 \\ -\ 5\ 2\ 3 \\ \hline \end{array}$$

11.
$$\begin{array}{r} 6\ 9\ 2 \\ -\ 4\ 8\ 3 \\ \hline \end{array}$$

12.
$$\begin{array}{r} 9\ 0\ 9 \\ -\ 7\ 3\ 8 \\ \hline \end{array}$$

13.
$$\begin{array}{r} 6\ 5\ 4 \\ -\ 4\ 2\ 1 \\ \hline \end{array}$$

14.
$$\begin{array}{r} 8\ 4\ 6 \\ -\ 2\ 8\ 4 \\ \hline \end{array}$$

Y. 376	K. 562	T. 209	L. 376	H. 461
T. 25	I. 729	A. 361	D. 144	I. 171
S. 331	R. 191	C. 233	G. 172	

RIDDLE ME MATH!

Directions: Solve each math problem. Then find the answer and write the letter in the correct place to solve the riddles.

WHOEVER MAKES IT, TELLS IT NOT. WHOEVER TAKES IT, KNOWS IT NOT. WHOEVER KNOWS IT, WANTS IT NOT. WHAT IS IT?

C											
1	2	3	4	5	6	7	8	9	10	11	12

13	14	15	16 .

1
```
  1 1
  4 8 5
+ 8 5 9
-------
1 3 4 4
```

2
```
  6 4 7
- 3 2 6
-------
```

3
```
  2 7 3
+ 5 2 6
-------
```

4
```
  3 5 2
- 1 0 5
-------
```

5
```
  5 2 5
+ 3 7 2
-------
```

6
```
  9 3 8
- 7 4 4
-------
```

7
```
  7 6 9
+ 6 6 2
-------
```

8
```
  4 3 6
- 2 7 7
-------
```

9
```
  2 7 3
+ 4 8 8
-------
```

10
```
  8 2 5
- 5 6 2
-------
```

11
```
  3 4 8
+ 7 4 3
-------
```

12
```
  7 8 3
- 3 2 1
-------
```

13
```
  6 3 7
+ 1 8 5
-------
```

14
```
  7 0 9
- 4 3 7
-------
```

15
```
  2 6 3
+ 5 7 5
-------
```

16
```
  9 7 5
- 4 1 8
-------
```

E. 838	T. 897	N. 272	E. 194	U. 799	Y. 557	~~C. 1344~~ O. 822
O. 321	F. 159	I. 263	T. 1091	M. 462	R. 1431	N. 247 E. 761

DIVISION DUPLICATION
4TH GRADE

There are 7 pairs of matching cards. Solve the equations then draw a line between symbols with the matching answers in the key below.

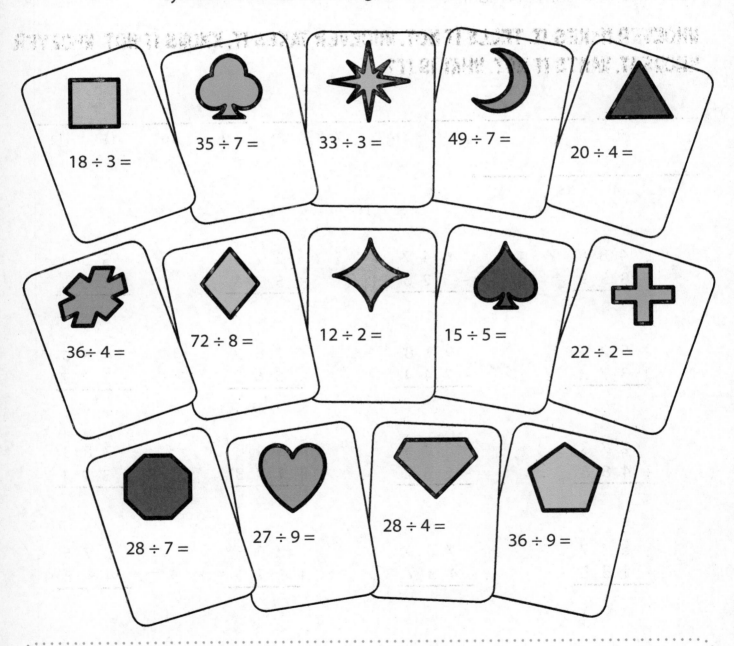

$18 \div 3 =$

$35 \div 7 =$

$33 \div 3 =$

$49 \div 7 =$

$20 \div 4 =$

$36 \div 4 =$

$72 \div 8 =$

$12 \div 2 =$

$15 \div 5 =$

$22 \div 2 =$

$28 \div 7 =$

$27 \div 9 =$

$28 \div 4 =$

$36 \div 9 =$

KEY:

Detective Zoey Chase is searching for Ruby Seeker throughout the Western United States after she escaped from jail in Spokane, Washington. Help Zoey follow Ruby by solving the following multiplication problems and drawing a line to each city and zip code where she steps in the order the problems are given.

1
```
    991
  x  99
```
```
   8,919
+ 89,190
```
Seattle 98,109

2
```
  1,417
  x   60
```

3
```
  4,262
  x   21
```

4
```
    457
  x 195
```

5
```
    469
  x 201
```

6
```
    544
  x 173
```

7
```
  1,993
  x   42
```

8
```
    460
  x 183
```

9
```
  1,217
  x   74
```

10
```
  4,861
  x   20
```

11
```
    691
  x 144
```

12
```
  2,239
  x   44
```

AK

Anchorage
99504

Seattle
98109

Olympia
98516

WA   Spokane

Portland
97220

OR   ID

Boise
83706

NV

Sacramento
94269

Reno
89502

Salt Lake City
84180

San Francisco
94112

CA   UT

Las Vegas
89115

Los Angeles
90058

AZ

Phoenix
85020

HI

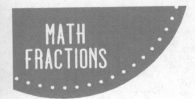

SKILL PRACTICE 1
FINDING THE GCF

The **greatest common factor (GCF)** is the largest whole number that divides evenly into multiple numbers. Look at the two numbers in each problem and find the greatest common factor between them. See the example below for a step by step process to finding the *GCF*.

EXAMPLE:

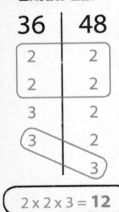

36	48
2	2
2	2
3	2
3	2
	3

$2 \times 2 \times 3 = \mathbf{12}$
GCF

$36 = 18 \times 2$
$36 = 9 \times 2 \times 2$
$36 = 3 \times 3 \times 2 \times 2$
$48 = 24 \times 2$
$48 = 12 \times 2 \times 2$
$48 = 6 \times 2 \times 2 \times 2$
$48 = 3 \times 2 \times 2 \times 2 \times 2$

2 is a prime number and divides into 18 evenly 36 times.

18 can be divided by 2, leaving 9.

9 can be divided by 3, leaving 3. Now we have all prime numbers.

Once you find the prime factors of the second number, see which numbers they have in common. Circle and multiply them to get your GCF. If there are no prime factors in common, then the GCF is 1.

Numbers in common: 2, 2, 3

40	60

GCF

30	75

GCF

84	105

GCF

56	96

GCF

18	25

GCF

50	125

GCF

72	108

GCF

56	112

GCF

BULL'S EYE MULTIPLY

Use multiplication to find the points awarded for hitting each zone. The outer red circle multiplies the number by 3 and the inner blue circle multiplies it by 7.

14

9

$$\begin{array}{r} 9 \\ \times\ 3 \\ \hline = \underline{27} \end{array}$$

3

21

12

$$\begin{array}{r} 9 \\ \times\ 7 \\ \hline = \underline{63} \end{array}$$

23

17

11

8

31

29

16

Look at the darts on the board. How many points were scored?

◯ + ◯ + ◯ = ◯

DIVISION
WORD PROBLEMS

1 Billy receives $15 every month for allowance. He puts $7 of his allowance into a piggy bank until his piggy bank has $119. How many months has he been saving part of his allowance?

2 Miss Amy collected $6 each from her students for their upcoming field trip. If all of her students went on the field trip she would collect $192. How many students are in Miss Amy's class?

3 Mr. Chong is also planning for his class to go on the same trip. He collects $6 from each of his students too, but one of his students could only pay $3 making his total $219. How many students are in his class?

4 Kari gets $20 every week for lunch money. She sets aside $2 every school day. How many weeks did it take for her to save up $65?

5 Susan is selling raffle tickets for $4. She collects a total of $284. How many tickets did she sell?

LEMONADE STAND MATH

You and your friends run a lemonade stand everyday during the summer. You are in charge of keeping track of the volume of lemonade sold. Given the number of cups sold each day, use division to express the number of cups sold in gallons, quarts, and cups.

Follow the example below. Refer to the **conversion box** to convert your units correctly. Show and check your work.

Conversion Box

Gal = Gallons
Qt = Quarts
C = Cups

1 Gal = 16 C
1 Qt = 4 C

MON.
Cups sold: 19

1st: Find the number of gallons using division.

$$1 G = 16 C \quad 16\overline{)19} \;\; R:3 \quad \frac{1}{-16}$$
$$3$$

1 Gal

2nd: Convert the remaining cups into quarts. The remainder is the number of cups left over.

$$1 Q = 4 C \quad 4\overline{)3} \;\; R:3 \quad \frac{0}{-0}$$
$$3$$

0 Qt

3 C

TUES. Cups sold: 23

WED. Cups sold: 50

THURS. Cups sold: 44

( ) Gal ( ) Qt ( ) C

( ) Gal ( ) Qt ( ) C

( ) Gal ( ) Qt ( ) C

FRI. Cups sold: 170

SAT. Cups sold: 134

SUN. Cups sold: 115

( ) Gal ( ) Qt ( ) C

( ) Gal ( ) Qt ( ) C

( ) Gal ( ) Qt ( ) C

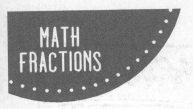
SKILL PRACTICE 3
FINDING THE GCF

The **greatest common factor (GCF)** is the largest whole number that divides evenly into multiple numbers. Look at the two numbers in each problem and find the greatest common factor between them. See the example below for a step by step process to finding the *GCF*.

EXAMPLE:

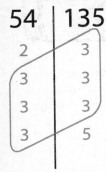

54	135
2	3
3	3
3	3
3	5

$54 = 27 \times 2$
$54 = 9 \times 3 \times 2$
$54 = 3 \times 3 \times 3 \times 2$

$135 = 27 \times 5$
$135 = 9 \times 3 \times 5$
$135 = 3 \times 3 \times 3 \times 5$

2 is a prime number and divides into 54 evenly 27 times.

27 can be divided by 3, leaving 9.

9 can be divided by 3, leaving 3. Now we have all prime numbers.

Once you find the prime factors of the second number, see which numbers they have in common. Circle and multiply them to get your GCF. If there are no prime factors in common, then the GCF is 1.

Numbers in common: 3, 3, 3

$3 \times 3 \times 3 = \textbf{27}$
GCF

36	54

GCF

60	210

GCF

16	64

GCF

56	84

GCF

48	120

GCF

22	49

GCF

15	75

GCF

24	84

GCF

GREATER THAN OR LESS THAN?

> "GREATER THAN"   < "LESS THAN"   = "EQUAL"

Direction: Solve the equations then write down the symbol that best compares each answer. Then write the answer in word form.

Example: (232 x 32) $>$ (22 x 150)   Seven thousand, four hundred and twenty-four is
                7424   3300   greater than three thousand, three hundred.

1
$$539 \times 223 \quad \bigcirc \quad 133 \times 624$$

....
....
....
....

2
$$439 \times 173 \quad \bigcirc \quad 244 \times 324$$

....
....
....
....

3
$$453 \times 513 \quad \bigcirc \quad 1223 \times 154$$

....
....
....
....

3
$$745 \times 16 \quad \bigcirc \quad 394 \times 85$$

....
....
....
....

#1

PRACTICE FINDING THE VARIABLE

A variable represents the unknown number in the equation. For example, $4 \times t = 12$. The letter "t" represents the number which multiplies by 4 to equal 12. Find the value of each variable in these equations. See the example below.

1 $6 \times j = 30$ $j =$ $\boxed{30 \div 6}$ $j =$ $\boxed{5}$

2 $8 \times b = 32$ $b =$ $\boxed{}$ $b =$ $\boxed{}$

3 $9 \times u = 63$ $u =$ $\boxed{}$ $u =$ $\boxed{}$

4 $11 \times e = 55$ $e =$ $\boxed{}$ $e =$ $\boxed{}$

5 $22 \times k = 44$ $k =$ $\boxed{}$ $k =$ $\boxed{}$

6 $d \times 5 = 100$ $d =$ $\boxed{}$ $d =$ $\boxed{}$

7 $h \times 20 = 400$ $h =$ $\boxed{}$ $h =$ $\boxed{}$

SODOKU ISLAND

Solve the Sudoku puzzle by filling in the blank spaces with numbers between 1 and 9. Make sure no numbers appear twice in the same row, column or 3x3 square.

DIFFICULTY; MEDIUM

	6	2	9	8	7			1
9	8		3		5	6	4	
7	3	5		1			9	2
3		9	8	6	4		1	
8	7	6	1		3	9	2	4
	5		2	7	9	3		8
2	4			9		1	5	6
	9	7	6		1		8	3
6			5	3	2	4	7	

MATH GO ROUND

Multiplication I Difficulty:
★★★★★

Find a friend and practice your multiplication skills.
Find two coins or game pieces and place them on the
square labeled **START**. Choose one of the problems
to solve and move your game piece clockwise around
the board to that problem's answer.

Keep track of the number of corners you go around
on each move. For each one, give yourself a point. The
player with the most points at the end is the winner.

Keep score with the table below.

	PLAYER 1	PLAYER 2
Round 1		
Round 2		
Round 3		
Round 4		
Round 5		
Round 6		
Round 7		
Round 8		

TOTAL _____

START · +1 Point

+1 Point

Top row: 850 · 208 · 216 · 350

Left column: 169 · 140 · 2,107 · 456

Right column: 690 · 4,602 · 1,755 · 837

Bottom row: 840 · 1,820 · 1,376 · 256

Problems (inner grid):

$$\begin{array}{r} 13 \\ \times 13 \end{array} \qquad \begin{array}{r} 42 \\ \times 20 \end{array} \qquad \begin{array}{r} 16 \\ \times 13 \end{array} \qquad \begin{array}{r} 25 \\ \times 14 \end{array}$$

$$\begin{array}{r} 18 \\ \times 12 \end{array} \qquad \begin{array}{r} 14 \\ \times 10 \end{array} \qquad \begin{array}{r} 45 \\ \times 39 \end{array} \qquad \begin{array}{r} 50 \\ \times 17 \end{array}$$

$$\begin{array}{r} 78 \\ \times 59 \end{array} \qquad \begin{array}{r} 16 \\ \times 16 \end{array} \qquad \begin{array}{r} 65 \\ \times 28 \end{array} \qquad \begin{array}{r} 30 \\ \times 23 \end{array}$$

$$\begin{array}{r} 49 \\ \times 43 \end{array} \qquad \begin{array}{r} 31 \\ \times 27 \end{array} \qquad \begin{array}{r} 43 \\ \times 32 \end{array} \qquad \begin{array}{r} 24 \\ \times 19 \end{array}$$

+1 Point · +1 Point

Great Job!

is an Education.com math superstar

ANSWERS

Addition Facts

Multiplication problems can also be expressed with addition. Write the addition facts that go with each multiplication sentence. The first one is done for you.

3 x 7 = $\underline{3 + 3 + 3 + 3 + 3 + 3 + 3}$

5 x 4 = $\underline{5 + 5 + 5 + 5}$

6 x 2 = $\underline{6 + 6}$

10 x 5 = $\underline{10 + 10 + 10 + 10 + 10}$

7 x 7 = $\underline{7 + 7 + 7 + 7 + 7 + 7 + 7}$

9 x 4 = $\underline{9 + 9 + 9 + 9}$

Look at the pictures below.

Write the addition fact: $\underline{2 + 2 + 2 + 2 + 2}$

Write the multiplication sentence: $\underline{2 \times 5}$

page 3

Making Multiplication Sentences

Look at each picture below. Write both the addition and multiplication facts that illustrate each picture. The first one is done for you.

$2 + 2 + 2$	$1 + 1 + 1 + 1$
$2 \times 3 = 6$	$1 \times 4 = 4$

$3 + 3 + 3$	$5 + 5 + 5 + 5$
$3 \times 3 = 9$	$5 \times 4 = 20$

$4 + 4 + 4 + 4 + 4 + 4$

$4 \times 6 = 24$

page 4

Making Multiplication Sentences

 Kick off! Time to take the field and score a touchdown for the home team. Solve the following multiplication problems and you'll be an All-Pro! **#1**

3 x 8 = $\underline{24}$ 6 x 4 = $\underline{24}$ 3 x 7 = $\underline{21}$ 9 x 2 = $\underline{18}$

4 x 3 = $\underline{12}$ 5 x 5 = $\underline{25}$ 7 x 2 = $\underline{14}$ 4 x 4 = $\underline{16}$

5 x 1 = $\underline{5}$ 3 x 3 = $\underline{9}$ 2 x 4 = $\underline{8}$ 5 x 2 = $\underline{10}$

1 x 6 = $\underline{6}$ 4 x 5 = $\underline{20}$ 2 x 6 = $\underline{12}$ 3 x 5 = $\underline{15}$

page 5

Making Multiplication Sentences

 Kick off! Time to take the field and score a touchdown for the home team. Solve the following multiplication problems and you'll be an All-Pro! **#2**

6 x 4 = $\underline{24}$ 7 x 2 = $\underline{14}$ 3 x 5 = $\underline{15}$ 8 x 1 = $\underline{8}$

3 x 3 = $\underline{9}$ 2 x 8 = $\underline{16}$ 7 x 3 = $\underline{21}$ 4 x 2 = $\underline{8}$

8 x 3 = $\underline{24}$ 4 x 5 = $\underline{20}$ 6 x 2 = $\underline{12}$ 9 x 1 = $\underline{9}$

7 x 8 = $\underline{56}$ 1 x 8 = $\underline{8}$ 9 x 3 = $\underline{27}$ 3 x 4 = $\underline{12}$

page 6

Making Multiplication Sentences

Kick off! Time to take the field and score a touchdown for the home team. Solve the following multiplication problems and you'll be an All-Pro!

#3

2 × 9 = 18   3 × 3 = 9   5 × 0 = 0   8 × 3 = 24

5 × 2 = 10   7 × 3 = 21   2 × 2 = 4   7 × 1 = 7

4 × 3 = 12   8 × 2 = 16   5 × 5 = 25   6 × 3 = 18

9 × 5 = 45   4 × 4 = 16   2 × 3 = 6   4 × 1 = 4

page 7

Making Multiplication Sentences

Kick off! Time to take the field and score a touchdown for the home team. Solve the following multiplication problems and you'll be an All-Pro!

#4

5 × 2 = 10   6 × 3 = 18   2 × 2 = 4   8 × 2 = 16

4 × 5 = 20   2 × 7 = 14   1 × 8 = 8   3 × 4 = 12

6 × 4 = 24   3 × 3 = 9   3 × 5 = 15   6 × 2 = 12

4 × 5 = 20   2 × 4 = 8   1 × 3 = 3   4 × 8 = 32

page 8

Making Multiplication Sentences

Kick off! Time to take the field and score a touchdown for the home team. Solve the following multiplication problems and you'll be an All-Pro!

#5

6 × 2 = 12   8 × 3 = 24   9 × 2 = 18   0 × 7 = 0

4 × 6 = 24   3 × 3 = 9   6 × 3 = 18   2 × 4 = 8

7 × 3 = 21   6 × 2 = 12   1 × 9 = 9   5 × 5 = 25

2 × 5 = 20   3 × 1 = 8   6 × 3 = 3   9 × 8 = 72

page 9

Find The Multiplication Facts

Multiplication is the reverse of division.
Example: If the division sentence is 12 ÷ 6 = 2,
Then the related multiplication facts are 6 × 2 = 12 and 2 × 6 = 12.
Look at these division sentences, and write down the two related multiplication facts.

10 ÷ 5 = 2
5 x 2 = 10
2 x 5 = 10

35 ÷ 7 = 5
7 x 5 = 35
5 x 7 = 35

96 ÷ 8 = 12
12 x 8 = 96
8 x 12 = 96

120 ÷ 12 = 10
12 x 10 = 120
10 x 12 = 120

44 ÷ 11 = 4
11 x 4 = 44
4 x 11 = 44

76 ÷ 2 = 38
12 x 8 = 96
8 x 12 = 96

81 ÷ 9 = 9
9 x 9 = 81
9 x 9 = 81

75 ÷ 25 = 3
25 x 3 = 75
3 x 25 = 75

999 ÷ 3 = 333
3 x 333 = 999
333 x 3 = 999

page 10   89

Umbrella Math

Complete each math problem and color the page.

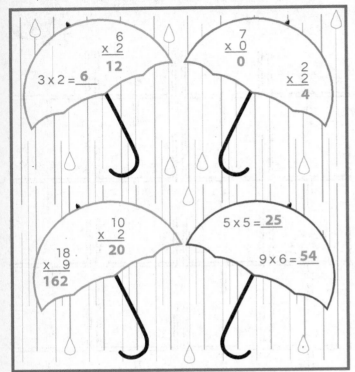

$$\begin{array}{r} 6 \\ \times\ 2 \\ \hline 12 \end{array}$$

$$3 \times 2 = \underline{6}$$

$$\begin{array}{r} 7 \\ \times\ 0 \\ \hline 0 \end{array}$$

$$\begin{array}{r} 2 \\ \times\ 2 \\ \hline 4 \end{array}$$

$$\begin{array}{r} 10 \\ \times\ 2 \\ \hline 20 \end{array}$$

$$\begin{array}{r} 18 \\ \times\ 9 \\ \hline 162 \end{array}$$

$$5 \times 5 = \underline{25}$$

$$9 \times 6 = \underline{54}$$

page 11

Apple Tree Math

Complete each math problem and color the page.

$$\begin{array}{r} 19 \\ \times\ 10 \\ \hline 190 \end{array}$$

$$\begin{array}{r} 25 \\ \times\ 10 \\ \hline 250 \end{array}$$

$$\begin{array}{r} 6 \\ \times\ 3 \\ \hline 18 \end{array}$$

$$\begin{array}{r} 28 \\ \times\ 13 \\ \hline 364 \end{array}$$

$$\begin{array}{r} 22 \\ \times\ 11 \\ \hline 242 \end{array}$$

$$\begin{array}{r} 8 \\ \times\ 5 \\ \hline 40 \end{array}$$

$$\begin{array}{r} 9 \\ \times\ 2 \\ \hline 18 \end{array}$$

page 12

Mammoth Multiplication Problems

There is no monkeying around with these multiplication problems!

72 × 3 = 216	43 × 6 = 258	28 × 2 = 56	38 × 8 = 304
55 × 4 = 220	19 × 9 = 171	63 × 7 = 441	78 × 5 = 390
49 × 6 = 294	82 × 3 = 246	57 × 8 = 456	15 × 4 = 60
36 × 7 = 252	67 × 2 = 134	22 × 9 = 198	89 × 5 = 445

90   **page 13**

Double Digit Multiplication

They may look tough but, you can do these double digit multiplication problems!

34 × 45 = 1530	78 × 42 = 3276	94 × 12 = 1128	14 × 33 = 462
56 × 77 = 4312	84 × 24 = 2016	16 × 51 = 816	65 × 11 = 715
76 × 20 = 1520	30 × 62 = 1860	22 × 99 = 2178	89 × 47 = 4183

page 14

> "Greater Than"   < "Less Than"   = "Equal"

Directions: Solve the equations then write down the symbol that best compares each answer. Then write the answer in word form

Example:
232 x 32 **>** 22 x 150
7424   3300

Seven thousand, four hundred and twenty-four is greater than three thousand, three hundred.

1. 89
   x 63   **>**   134
          x 24
   5607   **3216**

Five thousand, six hundred and seven is greater than three thousand, two hundred and sixteen.

2. 346
   x 3   **>**   45
          x 23
   1038   **1035**

One thousand and thirty-eight is greater than one thousand and thirty-five.

3. 142
   x 10   **=**   71
          x 20
   1420   **1420**

One thousand, four hundred and twenty is equal to one thousand, four hundred and twenty.

4. 232
   x 85   **<**   560
          x 42
   19,720   **23,520**

Nineteen thousand, seven hundred and twenty is less than twenty-three thousand, five hundred and twenty.

5. 843
   x 27   **>**   235
          x 94
   22,761   **22090**

Twenty-two thousand, seven hundred and sixty-one is greater than twenty two thousand and ninety.

page 15

> "Greater Than"   < "Less Than"   = "Equal"

Directions: Solve the equations then write down the symbol that best compares each answer. Then write the answer in word form

Example:
232 x 32 **>** 22 x 150
7424   3300

Seven thousand, four hundred and twenty-four is greater than three thousand, three hundred.

1. 539
   x 223   **>**   133
           x 624
   120,197   **82,992**

One hundred twenty thousand, one hundred and ninety-seven is greater than eighty-two thousand, nine hundred and ninety-two.

2. 439
   x 173   **<**   244
           x 324
   75,947   **79,056**

Seventy-five thousand, nine hundred fortyseven is less than seventy-nine thousand, and fifty-six.

3. 453
   x 513   **>**   1223
            x 154
   232,389   **188,342**

Two hundred, thirty-two thousand, three hundred and eighty-nine is greater than one hundred eighty-eight thousand, three hundred and forty-two.

4. 745
   x 16   **<**   394
          x 85
   11,920   **33,490**

Eleven thousand, nine hundred and twenty is less than thirty-three thousand, four hundred and ninety.

page 16

Multiplication Word Problems

Math isn't just for math class. It is used to solve problems in every subject. Help Mr. Hammond's class figure out their problems using math. Show your work.

Henry wants to see how many different colored crayons are in the crayon box. If there here are 4 rows of 19 crayons, how many different colors are there?

```
     19
   x  4
     76
```

76 crayons

Mikey is typing in the computer lab and typing at 23 words per minute. If he types for 11 minutes, how many words does he type?

```
     23
   x 11
```
253 words

All of the students have a vocabulary assignment every week with 13 new words. If the school year is 40 weeks long, how many new words will they learn?

```
        40
      x 13
       120
      +400
       520
```
520 words

```
       23
     x 11
       23
     +230
       253
```

Jeremy is building a toothpick skyscraper. Look at the picture below of the first floor. How many tooth picks will it take to build 12 stories? How many marshmallows will it take to build 12 stories?

```
   16        40
  x12       x12
   32        80
 +160      +400
  192       480
```
480 toothpicks

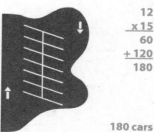

192 marshmallows

It's the day before Valentine's Day and Shelley needs to get Valentine cards for all of her classmates. The desks are arranged in a rectangle 7 rows wide and 5 rows long. If there are 3 desks that are empty, how many students are in the class?

```
       7
     x 5
      35
```
32 students   35 - 3 = 32

page 17

Merchandise Multiplication

Use multiplication to solve the following problems. Show your work.

The Nguyen family gets movies from Movie Mail home video delivery service. They get 3 movies at the beginning of the week and return them at the end of each week. If they continue this pattern, how many movies will they see in one year? (1 year = 52 weeks)

3 x 52 = 156

156 movies

Look at the diagram of a portion of the local grocery store's parking lot. If there are 15 rows of parking spaces in the lot like this one, how many cars can the park-ing lot fit in total?

```
       12
     x 15
       60
     +120
       180
```
180 cars

Mr. Hayes is having friends over to watch basketball and needs to buy snacks. He buys 5 boxes of crackers. In each box there are 3 sleeves of 24 crackers. How many crackers did he buy all together? This is a two step problem. Try multiplying the numbers in different orders. Do you get the same answer?   *You can find this answer by multiplying the numbers in any order.

24 x 3 = 72
72 x 5 = 360

360 crackers

Mr. Chang is comparing television screen sizes. Screen #1 is 18 by 23 inches and screen #2 is 19 by 22 inches. Which television has the larger screen?

```
       18        19
     x 23       x 22
       54        38
     +360      +380
      414       418
```
Screen #2

page 18

Wild Word Problems

Math in the animal kingdom! Use multiplication to solve the following problems. Add or subtract when necessary. Show your work.

Mario walks his dog every day. The walk path makes a giant loop that is 279 feet long. If Mario and his dog make 3 laps around the loop, how far do they walk?

279 x 3 = 837
They walk 837 feet long.

Racquel buys a small aquarium for her fish collection. The fish tank is 27 inches wide, 13 inches tall, and 13 inches deep. What is the maximum volume of water can the aquarium hold? This is problem requires two multiplication steps, does the order of operations matter? Remember, Volume = Length x Width x Height.

Volume = 27 x 13 x 13
= 4,563 cubic inches
Order of operation does not matter.

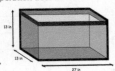

Josefina's cat, Whiskers, climbed into a tree and was too scared to come down. Her dad climbed up a ladder to bring down Whiskers. If Josefina's dad had to climb up 15 ladder steps and the steps are 32 centimeters apart, how high up did Whiskers go?

15 x 32 = 480
Whiskers went up 480 cms.

Julie is teaching her parrot, Romeo, how to say new words. If she teaches him 11 words each month. How many words will Romeo learn in a year?

11 x 12 = 132
Romeo will learn 132 words in a year.

Family Vacation Multiplication

The Smiths are going on a family vacation. Use multiplication, addition, and subtraction to solve the following problems. Perform other operations as needed to help find the answers. Show your work.

Driving to the airport, the Smiths needed to fill up on gasoline. Gasoline costs 3 dollars for one gallon. If their tank holds 16 gallons, and they already have 3 gallons filled, how much money will it cost to fill the car's tank completely?

(16 gallons - 3 gallons) = 13 gallons
13 x $3 per gallon = $39
It cost $39 to fill the tank completely.

The Smiths want to visit a museum and must pay to park. They are going to be gone for 4 hours. The price of parking is as follows:
1 Quarter = 15 minutes
1 Dime = 5 minutes
1 Nickel = 2 minutes
The Smiths have 8 quarters, 12 dimes and 14 nickels. Do they have enough to park for 4 hours? (Remember: 60 minutes = 1 hour)

15 min. x 8 quarters = 120 min.
5 min. x 12 dimes = 60 min.
2 min. x 14 nickels = 28 min.
120 + 60 + 128 = 3 hours & 28 min.
The Smiths do not have enough money to park for 4 hours.

The Smiths board the airplane to head back home. The flight attendant wants to count how many passengers are on board. Every row consists of 2, 3, and 2 seats each (see picture below). If there are 51 horizontal rows, and 13 seats are empty, how many passengers are on board?

51 rows x 7 seats = 357 seats total
357 - 13 = 344
There are 344 passengers on board.

In total, the Smiths were flying in an airplane for 14 hours. If the airplane cruises at approximately 512 miles per hour, about how many miles did they travel all together?

14 hours x 512 miles = 7,168
They traveled 7,168 miles.

Finding Factors

Factors are numbers that you multiply together to get another number. For example, 2 multiplied by 4 equals 8. So 2 and 4 are the factors of 8. Find the factors of the numbers below. See the example.

10 = **2 x 5**   18 = **3 x 6**

24 = **4 x 6**   30 = **5 x 6**

32 = **4 x 8**   39 = **3 x 13**

Find the missing factors.

15 = 3 x **5**   21 = 3 x **7**

45 = 9 x **5**   42 = 7 x **6**

36 = 2 x 2 x 3 x **3**

60 = 2 x 3 x 2 x **5**

75 = 5 x 3 x **5**

*When the factor is a prime number, it is called a prime factor.

Multiply Three Numbers

Here's a trick! First, multiply the first number by the second one. Then multiply the product of the first two numbers by the third number. Find the product of these multiplication sentences. The first one is done for you.

3 x 6 x 2	5 x 4 x 3
18 x 2	**20** x 3
36	60

2 x 4 x 6	3 x 5 x 3
8 x 6	**15** x 3
48	45

4 x 3 x 2 x 2	6 x 5 x 4 x 3
12 x 2 x 2	**30** x 4 x 3
24 x 2	**120** x 3
48	360

Math-Go-Round

Multiplication | Difficulty: ★★★★

Find a friend and practice your multiplication skills. Find two coins or game pieces and place them on the square labeled START. Choose one of the problems to solve and move your game piece clockwise around the board to that problem's answer. Keep track of the number of corners you go around on each move. For each one, give yourself a point. The player with the most points at the end is the winner. Keep score with the table below.

	Player 1	Player 2
Round 1		
Round 2		
Round 3		
Round 4		
Round 5		
Round 6		
Round 7		
Round 8		
Total		

Game Board

Top row: +1 Point (corner), 1,610, 3,021, 8,840, 8,772, +1 Point (corner)

Left column (top to bottom): 6,384, 4,462, 3,861, 7,957

Right column (top to bottom): 1,419, 9,322, 8,631, 3,336

Bottom row: START / +1 Point (corner), 1,694, 2,916, 4,653, 9,860, +1 Point (corner)

Center problems:

$$137 \times 63 = 8{,}631$$
$$104 \times 85 = 8{,}840$$
$$158 \times 59 = 9{,}322$$
$$159 \times 19 = 3{,}021$$

$$141 \times 33 = 4{,}653$$
$$115 \times 14 = 1{,}610$$
$$139 \times 24 = 3{,}336$$
$$108 \times 27 = 2{,}916$$

$$152 \times 42 = 6{,}384$$
$$194 \times 23 = 4{,}462$$
$$170 \times 58 = 9{,}860$$
$$109 \times 73 = 7{,}957$$

$$143 \times 27 = 3{,}861$$
$$172 \times 51 = 8{,}772$$
$$154 \times 11 = 1{,}694$$
$$129 \times 11 = 1{,}419$$

Odd One Out   page 29

1. 2   4. 2/20

2. 3/6   5. 36/63

3. 8/70   6. 3/6

Fraction Addition   page 30

A. 3/9 + 5/9 = 8/9

B. 4/9 + 2/9 = 6/9 or 2/3

C. 8/9 + 3/9 = 11/9 or1 2/9

D. 1/9 + 6/9 = 7/9

E. 17/12 or 1 5/12

F. 5/5 or 1

G. 5/4 or 1 1/4

H. 11/9 or 1 2/9

I. 19/12 or 1 7/12

J. 22/15 or 1 7/15

Simple Sherwin   page 31

1. 2/3   6. 1/2

2. 1/5   7. 4/5

3. 3/4   8. 1/2

4. 2/3   9. 2/5

5. 1/3   10. 3/5

Simple Sylvia   page 32

1. 1/4   6. 1/3

2. 2/3   7. 2/5

3. 1/2   8. 1/4

4. 3/4   9. 1/5

5. 1/2   10. 2/3

Simple Scooter   page 33

1. 3/4   6. 2/3

2. 1/5   7. 1/4

3. 4/5   8. 2/3

4. 1/2   9. 1/4

5. 3/4   10. 4/5

Steer and Simplify #1   page 34

1. 9/54 = 1/6
2. 6/15 = 2/5
3. 6/8 = 3/4
4. 27/45 = 3/5
5. 16/24 = 2/3
6. 24/27 = 8/9
7. 35/84 = 5/12
8. 18/60 = 3/10
9. 15/30 = 1/2
10. 5/40 = 1/8
11. 32/40 = 4/5
12. 4/6 = 2/3
13. 9/18 = 1/2
14. 28/40 = 7/10
15. 9/27 = 1/3
16. 40/55 = 8/11

Steer and Simplify #3   page 36

1. 4/20 = 1/5
2. 6/36 = 1/6
3. 18/45 = 2/5
4. 7/49 = 1/7
5. 4/6 = 2/3
6. 10/14 = 5/7
7. 27/90 = 3/10
8. 25/55 = 5/11
9. 3/9 = 1/3
10. 24/27 = 8/9
11. 20/25 = 4/5
12. 15/21 = 5/7
13. 10/15 = 2/3
14. 9/45 = 1/5
15. 4/8 = 1/2
16. 35/45 = 7/9

Steer and Simplify #2   page 35

1. 15/40 = 3/8
2. 27/90 = 3/10
3. 5/60 = 1/12
4. 12/42 = 2/7
5. 12/30 = 2/5
6. 27/63 = 3/7
7. 8/16 = 1/2
8. 7/63 = 1/9
9. 2/16 = 1/8
10. 30/55 = 6/11
11. 7/14 = 1/2
12. 15/24 = 5/8
13. 11/55 = 1/5
14. 12/54 = 2/9
15. 8/12 = 2/3
16. 49/70 = 7/10

Steer and Simplify #4   page 37

1. 6/15 = 2/5
2. 5/35 = 1/7
3. 4/40 = 1/10
4. 4/48 = 1/12
5. 8/40 = 1/5
6. 15/33 = 5/11
7. 5/30 = 1/6
8. 7/21 = 1/3
9. 2/8 = 1/4
10. 9/12 = 3/4
11. 3/6 = 1/2
12. 28/32 = 7/8
13. 5/10 = 1/2
14. 18/66 = 3/11
15. 42/60 = 7/10
16. 2/24 = 1/12

Skill Practice - Simplifying Fractions #1   page 38

1. 15/30 = 1/2
2. 16/80 = 1/5
3. 18/24 = 3/4
4. 45/54 = 5/6
5. 55/66 = 5/6
6. 18/72 = 1/4

7. 14/42 = 1/3
8. 27/54 = 1/2
9. 35/50 = 7/10
10. 19/30 ≈ 2/3
11. 14/41 ≈ 1/3
12. 20/81 ≈ 1/4

13. 24/49 ≈ 1/2
14. 17/80 ≈ 1/5
15. 27/37 ≈ 3/4
16. 23/72 ≈ 1/3
17. 13/21 ≈ 2/3
18. 99/100 ≈ 1

Skill Practice - Simplifying Fractions #2   page 39

1. 22/66 = 1/3
2. 15/20 = 3/4
3. 28/42 = 2/3
4. 12/36 = 1/3
5. 28/35 = 4/5
6. 23/46 = 1/2

7. 19/76 = 1/4
8. 18/60 = 3/10
9. 23/46 = 1/2
10. 45/51 ≈ 9/10
11. 11/45 ≈ 1/4
12. 13/24 ≈ 1/2

13. 23/30 ≈ 4/5
14. 89/90 ≈ 1
15. 31/36 ≈ 8/9
16. 37/72 ≈ 1/2
17. 49/64 ≈ 3/4
18. 10/61 ≈ 1/6

Skill Practice - Simplifying Fractions #3   page 40

1. 12/30 = 2/5
2. 20/24 = 5/6
3. 63/70 = 9/10
4. 5/15 = 1/3
5. 27/45 = 3/5
6. 10/20 = 1/2

7. 3/18 = 1/6
8. 18/27 = 2/3
9. 24/32 = 3/4
10. 16/63 ≈ 1/4
11. 75/99 ≈ 3/4
12. 13/25 ≈ 1/2

13. 19/100 ≈ 1/5
14. 11/72 ≈ 1/6
15. 41/63 ≈ 2/3
16. 28/71 ≈ 2/5
17. 24/99 ≈ 1/4
18. 19/98 ≈ 1/5

Feed the Kramsters #1   page 41

1. 2

2. 3 3/4

3. 1 1/2

4. 2 4/5

5. 3 1/3

Feed the Kramsters #2   page 42

1. 4

2. 2 3/5

3. 3

4. 2 2/5

5. 3 1/2

Feed the Kramsters #3   page 43

1. 1 4/5

2. 1 1/2

3. 3 1/3

4. 1 1/2

5. 3 1/5

Feed the Kramsters #4   page 44

1. 2 1/2

2. 3

3. 2 1/5

4. 3 2/3

5. 2 1/2

Feed the Kramsters #5   page 45

1. 2

2. 1 3/4

3. 4

4. 2 1/5

5. 2 1/4

1.

2.

3.

4.

Ranking Fractions   page 47

1. 3/4, 1/2, 1/3, 6/24, 1/5

2. 1/1, (12/30 = 4/10), 8/24, 3/30

3. 14/14, 15/20, 5/8/ 3/6, 5/15

4. 50/50, 9/12, 7/10, 3/6, 2/20

5. 2, 1, 2/3, 50/100, 4/10

6. 5/6, 4/5, 3/4, 1/2, 1/3

Skills Practice 1: Rounding and Place Values

4.253	12.02	95.408
thousandths	hundredths	thousandths

0.021	10.5	8.506
thousandths	tenths	thousandths

8.52	9.321	50.2
hundredths	thousandths	tenths

89.8	4,512.3	88.22
tenths	tenths	hundredths

Tenths

8.231	45.128	0.981	2.012	16.061
8.2	45.1	1.0	2.0	16.1

Hundredths

8.2561	66.2135	0.8646	7.9843	52.1143
8.26	66.21	0.86	7.98	52.11

Thousandths

0.8643	6.5127	0.2155	7.4541	1.8950
0.864	6.513	0.216	7.454	1.895

Mixed

45.1952	0.2315	81.0053	90.550	0.0186
45.20	0.232	81.005	90.6	0.019

page 53

Skills Practice 2: Rounding and Place Values

90.3	1.57	8.6
tenths	hundredths	tenths

19.521	325.40	20.050
thousandths	hundredths	thousandths

34.8	18.629	4.21
tenths	thousandths	hundredths

99.016	16.52	7.1
thousandths	hundredths	tenths

Tenths

5.291	51.0526	4.832	65.247	1.366
5.3	51.1	4.8	65.2	1.4

Hundredths

8.2952	21.5061	84.9315	14.6147	8.4473
8.30	21.51	84.93	14.61	8.45

Thousandths

52.3615	0.2381	12.4534	9.0267	9.4125
52.362	0.238	12.453	9.027	9.413

Mixed

11.2543	25.8963	94.4135	6.3519	5.7082
11.25	25.9	94.414	6.35	5.7

page 54

Skills Practice 1: Addition with Decimals

16.2 + 9.05

```
  16.2
+ 9.05
-------
 25.25
```

2.513 + 19.61

```
  2.513
+ 19.61
--------
 22.123
```

24.9 + 5.73

```
  24.9
+ 5.73
-------
 30.63
```

72.52 + 0.214

```
 72.52
+ 0.214
--------
 72.734
```

2.83 + 1.994

```
  2.83
+ 1.994
-------
 4.824
```

243.1 + 3.07

```
 243.1
+ 3.07
-------
 246.17
```

1.203 + 16.48

```
  1.203
+ 16.48
--------
 17.683
```

14.63 + 12.9

```
 14.63
+ 12.9
-------
 27.53
```

10.5 + 3.481

```
  10.5
+ 3.481
-------
 13.981
```

37.53 + 22.8

```
 37.53
+ 22.8
-------
 60.33
```

1.358 + 250.2

```
  1.358
+ 250.2
--------
 251.558
```

0.53 + 64.095

```
  0.53
+ 64.095
--------
 64.625
```

page 55

Sheep Math

page 56

Skills Practice 1: Subtracting with Decimals

95.2 - 5.58
```
  95.20
-  5.58
  25.25
```

8.23 - 1.257
```
  8.230
- 1.257
  6.973
```

61.3 - 7.35
```
  61.30
-  7.35
  53.95
```

10.08 - 9.6
```
  10.08
-  9.60
   0.48
```

7.109 - 3.3
```
  7.109
- 3.300
  3.809
```

75.3 - 13.19
```
  75.30
- 13.19
  62.11
```

8.024 - 6.76
```
  8.024
- 6.760
  1.264
```

18.8 - 14.52
```
  18.80
- 14.52
   4.28
```

5.6 - 2.863
```
  5.600
- 2.863
  2.737
```

7.25 - 6.01
```
  7.25
- 6.01
  1.24
```

25.3 - 4.192
```
  25.300
-  4.192
  21.108
```

70.5 - 4.61
```
  70.50
-  4.61
  65.89
```

page 57

Skills Practice 2: Subtracting with Decimals

18.63 - 2.041
```
  18.630
-  2.041
  16.589
```

8.45 - 6.3
```
  8.45
- 6.30
  2.15
```

7.41 - 0.196
```
  7.410
- 0.196
  7.214
```

4.215 - 3.2
```
  4.215
- 3.200
  1.015
```

20.12 - 13.7
```
  20.12
- 13.70
   6.42
```

4.2 - 0.429
```
  4.200
- 0.429
  3.771
```

126.4 - 0.147
```
  126.400
-   0.147
  126.253
```

77.98 - 15.6
```
  77.98
- 15.60
  62.38
```

43.2 - 12.75
```
  43.20
- 12.75
  30.45
```

9.35 - 3.282
```
  9.350
- 3.282
  6.068
```

62.45 - 3.187
```
  62.450
-  3.187
  59.263
```

1.248 - 1.19
```
  1.248
- 1.190
  0.058
```

page 58

Conversation: Practice Ordering Decimals

3 — R — 9.09219

2 — E — 9.35

7 — D — 7.09345

5 — U — 8.03912

8 — E — 6.917

4 — S — 8.49461

6 — A — 7.201

1 — P — 10.0001

Jacob is trying to

P E R S U A D E **Jack.**

page 59

Fractions: Simple Pleasures Candy

Jelly Beans

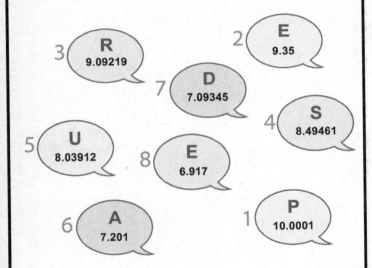

18 orange jelly beans — 45
$$\frac{18 \div 9}{45 \div 9} = \frac{2}{5}$$

21 blue jelly beans — 49
$$\frac{21 \div 7}{49 \div 7} = \frac{3}{7}$$

18 magenta jelly beans — 54
$$\frac{18 \div 9}{54 \div 9} = \frac{2}{6} = \frac{1}{3}$$

24 green jelly beans — 64
$$\frac{24 \div 8}{64 \div 8} = \frac{3}{8}$$

Candy Slices

45 magenta slices — 72
$$\frac{45 \div 9}{72 \div 9} = \frac{5}{8}$$

13 purple slices — 65
$$\frac{13 \div 13}{65 \div 13} = \frac{1}{5}$$

26 turquoise slices — 52
$$\frac{26 \div 13}{52 \div 13} = \frac{2}{4} = \frac{1}{2}$$

48 yellow slices — 84
$$\frac{48 \div 12}{84 \div 12} = \frac{4}{7}$$

Gummy Bears

21 yellow gummy bears — 84
$$\frac{21 \div 7}{84 \div 7} = \frac{3}{12} = \frac{1}{4}$$

12 red gummy bears — 40
$$\frac{12 \div 4}{40 \div 4} = \frac{3}{10}$$

26 green gummy bears — 63
$$\frac{26}{63}$$

5 orange gummy bears — 45
$$\frac{5 \div 5}{45 \div 5} = \frac{1}{9}$$

page 60

Fraction Action! Writing the Lowest Form: Take 1

Find the lowest form of the fractions below.
Write it down. Show your work.

$$\frac{4}{12} = \frac{4 \div 4}{12 \div 4} = \frac{1}{3}$$

$$\frac{5}{30} = \frac{5 \div 5}{30 \div 5} = \frac{1}{6}$$

$$\frac{8}{24} = \frac{8 \div 8}{24 \div 8} = \frac{1}{3}$$

Fill in the missing numerator or denominator.

$$\frac{7}{35} \div 7 = \frac{1}{5} \qquad \frac{3}{63} \div 3 = \frac{1}{21}$$

$$\frac{6}{36} \div 6 = \frac{1}{6} \qquad \frac{9}{33} \div 3 = \frac{3}{11}$$

page 61

Fraction Action! Writing the Lowest Form: Take 2

Look at the shading area on the left side. Write the fraction and then reduce it to the lowest form.

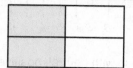 $= \frac{2}{4} = \frac{1}{2}$

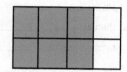 $= \frac{6}{8} = \frac{3}{4}$

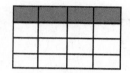 $= \frac{4}{16} = \frac{1}{4}$

Find the lowest form of the fraction below.

$$\frac{8}{36} = \frac{8 \div 4}{36 \div 4} = \frac{2}{9} \qquad \frac{6}{39} = \frac{6 \div 3}{39 \div 3} = \frac{2}{13}$$

page 62

The Greatest and the Least: Practicing Fractions

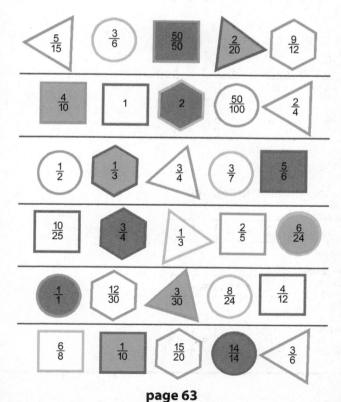

page 63

Colorful Shapes: Practicing Fractions

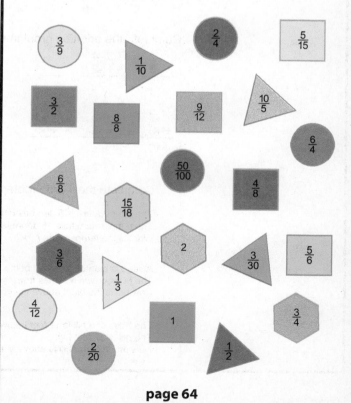

page 64

Introduction to Integers   page 65

Fill in the missing numbers to complete the number line.

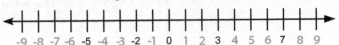

-9 -8 -7 -6 -5 -4 -3 -2 -1 0 1 2 3 4 5 6 7 8 9

Fill in the blanks with neutral, positive or negative.

Zero is a _____neutral_____ integer.

A whole number less than zero is a _____negative_____ integer.

A whole number greater than zero is a _____positive_____ integer.

Whole numbers that are _____positive_____ integers can be written with or without a sign.

Circle the integers

(-4)   ½   (3)   (-2)   (0)   ¾   (+6)   (8)   (-7)   ¼   (1)   (+9)

Match the opposite integers.

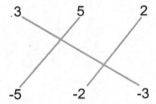

3   5   2

-5   -2   -3

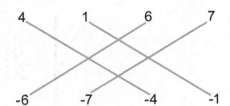

4   1   6   7

-6   -7   -4   -1

Adding Integers   page 66

Complete the number line.

-10 -9 -8 -7 -6 -5 -4 -3 -2 -1 0 1 2 3 4 5 6 7 8 9 10

Complete the addition problems.

-2	+4	+5	-6	+8	-1	-9
+ +3	+ -2	+ -1	+ +2	+ +2	+ -5	+ +8
+1	+2	+4	-4	+10	-6	-1

+7	-3	-4	+9	+6	-5	-4
+ +3	+ +6	+ +5	+ -7	+ -7	+ +6	+ -3
+10	+3	+1	+2	-1	+1	-7

Complete the word problems. Use the table to help you.

The temperature is 5 degrees below zero.
The temperature falls 15 degrees.
What is the temperature now?

-5	+	-15	=	-20

A seed is planted 2 inches below the ground.
The plant grows 6 inches from the seed.
How tall is the plant above the ground?

-2	+	+6	=	+4

The base of a hill is 11 feet below sea level.
The hill is 27 feet high.
How much of the hill is above sea level?

-11	+	+27	=	+16

Riddle Me Math! Multidigit Addition

What can you catch and not throw? A ___COLD___.

1. 1171   2. 800   3. 1306   4. 993

What kind of coat can only be put on when wet?
A ___COAT OF PAINT___.

5. 1022   6. 1445   7. 369   8. 700   9. 893

10. 1409   11. 1106   12. 1556   13. 1084   14. 1205

15. 471

page 71

Division Duplication: 4th Grade

$18 \div 3 = 6$ $35 \div 7 = 5$ $33 \div 3 = 11$ $49 \div 7 = 7$

$20 \div 4 = 5$ $36 \div 4 = 9$ $72 \div 8 = 9$ $12 \div 2 = 6$

$15 \div 5 = 3$ $22 \div 2 = 11$ $28 \div 7 = 4$ $27 \div 9 = 3$

$28 \div 4 = 7$ $36 \div 9 = 4$

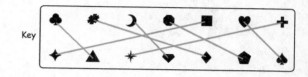

page 74

Riddle Me Math! Multidigit Subtraction

What can fill a room but takes up no space?
A ___LIGHT___.

1. 376   2. 729   3. 172   4. 461   5. 25

What has a foot on each side and one in the middle? A ___YARDSTICK___.

6. 376   7. 361   8. 191   9. 144   10. 331

11. 209   12. 171   13. 233   14. 562

page 72

Zoey Chase is on the Case!

1.
```
    991
  x  99
  8,919
+ 89,190
 98,109
```
Seattle

2.
```
  1,417
  x  60
      0
+ 85,020
 85,020
```
Phoenix

3.
```
  4,262
  x   21
  4,262
+ 85,240
 89,502
```
Reno

4.
```
    457
  x 195
  2,285
 41,130
+ 45,700
 89,115
```
Las Vegas

5.
```
    469
  x 201
    469
+ 93,800
 94,269
```
Sacramento

6.
```
    544
  x 173
  1,632
 38,080
+ 54,400
 94,112
```
San Francisco

7.
```
  1,993
  x   42
  3,986
+ 79,720
 83,706
```
Boise

8.
```
    460
  x 183
  1,380
 36,800
+ 46,000
 84,180
```
Salt Lake City

9.
```
  1,217
  x   74
  4,868
+ 85,190
 90,058
```
Los Angeles

10.
```
  4,861
  x   20
      0
+ 97,220
 97,220
```
Portland

11.
```
    691
  x 144
  2,764
 27,640
+ 69,100
 99,504
```
Anchorage

12.
```
  2,239
  x   44
  8,956
+ 89,560
 98,516
```
Olympia

* Answer key continuation on next page

page 75

Riddle Me Math! Multidigit Addition and Subtraction

Whoever makes it, tells it not. Whoever takes it, knows it not. Whoever knows it, wants it not. What is it? ___COUNTERFEIT MONEY___

1. 1344   2. 321   3. 799   4. 247   5. 897

6. 194   7. 1431   8. 159   9. 761   10. 263

11. 1091   12. 462   13. 822   14. 272   15. 836

16. 557

page 73

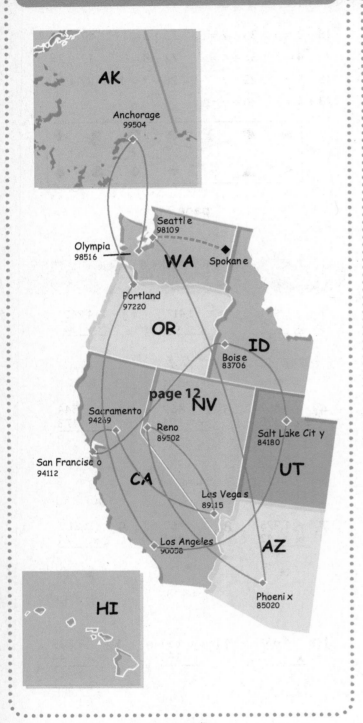

AK

Anchorage
99504

Seattle
98109

Olympia
98516

WA

Spokane

Portland
97220

OR

ID

Boise
83706

page 12

NV

Sacramento
94269

Reno
89502

Salt Lake City
84180

San Francisco
94112

CA

UT

Los Vegas
89115

Los Angeles
90058

AZ

Phoenix
85020

HI

Skill Practice 1

40	60
2	2
2	2
2	3
5	5

20

GCF

30	75
2	3
3	5
5	5

15

GCF

84	105
2	3
2	5
3	7
7	

21

GCF

56	96
2	2
2	2
2	2
7	2
	2
	3

8

GCF

18	25
2	5
3	5
3	

1

GCF

50	125
2	5
5	5
5	5

25

GCF

* Answer key continuation on next page

Skill Practice 1 (continuation)

72 | 108   56 | 112

2	2		2	2
2	2		2	2
2	3		2	2
3	3		7	2
3	3			7

36
GCF

28
GCF

page 76

Bulls' Eye Multiply

| 14 x 3 = 42 | 3 x 3 = 9 | 12 x 3 = 36 | 17 x 3 = 51 |
| 14 x 7 = 98 | 3 x 7 = 21 | 12 x 7 = 84 | 17 x 7 = 119 |

| 8 x 3 = 24 | 29 x 3 = 87 | 16 x 3 = 48 | 31 x 3 = 93 |
| 8 x 7 = 56 | 29 x 7 = 203 | 16 x 7 = 112 | 31 x 7 = 217 |

| 11 x 3 = 33 | 23 x 3 = 69 | 21 x 3 = 63 | 9 x 3 = 27 |
| 11 x 7 = 77 | 23 x 7 = 161 | 21 x 7 = 147 | 9 x 7 = 63 |

Look at the darts on the board. How many points were scored?

9 + 56 + 33 = 98

page 77

Division Word Problems

1. 119 (amount saved) ÷ 7 (amount left from his allowance) = 17 months

It took Billy 17 months to save up $119 in his piggy pank.

2. 192 (total collected money) ÷ 6 (collected per student) = 32 students

There are 32 students in Miss Amy's class.

3. 219 (total collected money) + 3 (the missing due from one student) = 222

There are 37 students in Mr. Chong's class. 222 ÷ 6 (collected per student) = 37 students

4. $2 (allowance saved) x 5 (# school lunch days) = $10 (allowance saved in a week)

$65 (total saved) ÷ $10 (allowance saved in a week) = 6.5 weeks round up to 7

It took her 7 weeks to save 65 dollars.

5. $284 (collected total) ÷ $4 (price per raffle ticket) = 71 (tickets sold)

Susan sold 71 tickets.

page 78

Lemonade Stand Math 5

Tues. _1_ Gal _1_ Qt _3_ C   **Wed.** _3_ Gal _0_ Qt _2_ C   **Thurs.** _2_ Gal _3_ Qt _0_ C

Fri. _10_ Gal _2_ Qt _2_ C   **Sat.** _8_ Gal _1_ Qt _2_ C   **Sun.** _7_ Gal _0_ Qt _3_ C

page 79

36	54
2	2
2	3
3	3
3	3

GCF: 18

60	210
2	2
3	3
3	5
5	7

GCF: 30

16	64
2	2
2	2
2	2
2	2
	2
	2

GCF: 16

56	84
2	2
2	2
2	3
7	7

GCF: 28

48	120
2	2
2	2
2	2
2	3
3	5

GCF: 24

22	49
2	7
11	7

GCF: 1

15	75
3	3
5	5
	5

GCF: 15

24	84
2	2
2	2
2	3
3	7

GCF: 12

page 80

1. $120,197 > 82,992$
One hundred twenty thousand, one hundred and ninety-seven is greater than eighty-two thousand, nine hundred and ninety-two.

2. $75,947 < 79,056$
Seventy-five thousand, nine hundred forty-seven is less than seventy-nine thousand and fifty-six.

3. $232,389 > 188,342$
Two hundred, thirty-two thousand, three hundred and eighty-nine is greater than one hundred eighty-eight thousand, three hundred and forty-two.

4. $11,920 < 33,490$
Eleven thousand, nine hundred and twenty is less than thirty-three thousand, four hundred and ninety.

page 81

106

Practice Finding The Variable

b= 32 ÷ 8   **u**= 63 ÷ 9   **e**= 55 ÷ 11
b= 4   **u**= 7   **e**= 5

k= 44 ÷ 22   **d**= 100 ÷ 5   **h**= 400 ÷ 20
k= 2   **d**= 20   **h**= 20

page 82

Sudoku Island

4	6	2	9	8	7	5	3	1
9	8	1	3	2	5	6	4	7
7	3	5	4	1	6	8	9	2
3	2	9	8	6	4	7	1	5
8	7	6	1	5	3	9	2	4
1	5	4	2	7	9	3	6	8
2	4	3	7	9	8	1	5	6
5	9	7	6	4	1	2	8	3
6	1	8	5	3	2	4	7	9

page 83

Math-Go-Round

$$
\begin{array}{r} 25 \\ \times\ 14 \\ \hline 350 \end{array}
\qquad
\begin{array}{r} 16 \\ \times\ 13 \\ \hline 208 \end{array}
\qquad
\begin{array}{r} 42 \\ \times\ 20 \\ \hline 840 \end{array}
\qquad
\begin{array}{r} 13 \\ \times\ 13 \\ \hline 169 \end{array}
$$

$$
\begin{array}{r} 50 \\ \times\ 17 \\ \hline 850 \end{array}
\qquad
\begin{array}{r} 45 \\ \times\ 39 \\ \hline 1755 \end{array}
\qquad
\begin{array}{r} 14 \\ \times\ 10 \\ \hline 140 \end{array}
\qquad
\begin{array}{r} 18 \\ \times\ 12 \\ \hline 216 \end{array}
$$

$$
\begin{array}{r} 30 \\ \times\ 23 \\ \hline 690 \end{array}
\qquad
\begin{array}{r} 65 \\ \times\ 28 \\ \hline 1820 \end{array}
\qquad
\begin{array}{r} 16 \\ \times\ 16 \\ \hline 256 \end{array}
\qquad
\begin{array}{r} 78 \\ \times\ 59 \\ \hline 4602 \end{array}
$$

$$
\begin{array}{r} 24 \\ \times\ 19 \\ \hline 456 \end{array}
\qquad
\begin{array}{r} 43 \\ \times\ 32 \\ \hline 1376 \end{array}
\qquad
\begin{array}{r} 31 \\ \times\ 27 \\ \hline 837 \end{array}
\qquad
\begin{array}{r} 49 \\ \times\ 43 \\ \hline 2107 \end{array}
$$

page 84